The Cold Buffet

Elijah Young

methuen | drama

LONDON • NEW YORK • OXFORD • NEW DELHI • SYDNEY

METHUEN DRAMA
Bloomsbury Publishing Plc
50 Bedford Square, London, WC1B 3DP, UK
1385 Broadway, New York, NY 10018, USA
29 Earlsfort Terrace, Dublin 2, Ireland

BLOOMSBURY, METHUEN DRAMA and the Methuen
Drama logo are trademarks of Bloomsbury Publishing Plc

First published in Great Britain 2023

Cover image: Sasa Savic

Cover design: Solution Group

Bloomsbury Publishing Plc does not have any control over, or responsibility
for, any third-party websites referred to or in this book. All internet addresses
given in this book were correct at the time of going to press. The author and
publisher regret any inconvenience caused if addresses have changed or sites
have ceased to exist, but can accept no responsibility for any such changes.

A catalogue record for this book is available from the British Library.

A catalog record for this book is available from the Library of Congress.

ISBN: PB: 978-1-3504-5457-6
ePDF: 978-1-3504-5458-3
eBook: 978-1-3504-5459-0

Series: Modern Plays

Typeset by Mark Heslington Ltd, Scarborough, North Yorkshire

To find out more about our authors and books visit
www.bloomsbury.com and sign up for our newsletters.

A Live Theatre production

The
Cold Buffet

A delicious North East family saga

Thursday 5 – Saturday 28 October 2023

This playscript went to press before rehearsals were
completed and so may differ from the performance.

The Cold Buffet
By Elijah Young

CAST

Nick Blakeley	Ellis
Jane Holman	Evelyn
Amara Karan	Ayeesha
Jim Kitson	David
Beth Fletcher Morris	Max

CREATIVE & PRODUCTION TEAM

Elijah Young	Writer
Jack McNamara	Director
Alison Ashton	Designer
Drummond Orr	Lighting Designer
Adam P McCready	Sound Designer
David Flynn	Associate Sound Designer
Lou Duffy	Costume Supervisor
Craig Davidson	Stage Manager
Gabriela Oliver	Deputy Stage Manager
Drummond Orr	Production Manager
Taylor Howie	Technician

A truly delicious North East family saga

There's always something to celebrate!

A death, a marriage, a birth. Three major life events that happen over the course of five years to the McCarthy family.

Making an appearance at these get-togethers is the only time Ellis can muster the strength to visit home. Awkward small talk with his cousin, underlying tension with his dad and a passive aggressive grandma are a few things he prepares himself for. But, when true feelings start to be unearthed, is it time for Ellis to finally cut ties?

Life happens. People change. Yet the same old buffet remains.

The centrepiece of Live Theatre's 50th anniversary season is this epic and feverishly funny saga by rising star Elijah Young.

A word from writer Elijah Young

This is a play that has been brewing in my mind for some time. I knew I wanted to write about three things, family drama, cultural Catholicism and cold buffets.

I grew up in Middlesbrough, a town rich with culture. Catholicism made its home in Teesside, due to steelwork attracting Irish migrants in the nineteenth century, and it still lives on. I've always been interested in my Irish heritage and my childhood was full of family parties with mother's Catholic side of the family. The buffet table was not exciting to me as a kid, all the things I wanted to eat were sad looking and ice cold. The older I got, the more it fascinated me.

Though my inspiration is drawn from Middlesbrough, the story of the McCarthy's could be any working class Catholic family in the North East and this play explores the good, the bad, the ugly and the hilarious, that we all see in our own. Everyone's family adopts their own sort of culture, their own way of operating and sometimes it's unhealthy. But how do we shake it off? Families are weird. There's an expectation of unwavering loyalty decided purely by blood. A parent, brother, aunty, grandparent or whoever could say the cruellest and most hurtful things yet there's a contract you unknowingly signed which states you have to still love and respect them. There's a boldness in their behaviour because they think they can get away with it. This, of course, is the perfect playing ground for drama.

The first time I said the idea out loud was at the Live Theatre playwriting course, so it feels very full circle for it to be a part of the season of work for Live Theatre's 50th anniversary. Still early on in my writing career, I had a desire to try things that scared me. Playing around with time, telling a story in three acts, balancing a lot of characters' voices, to name a few. When I became an Associate Artist at Live Theatre, it felt like the right time to push myself and experiment as I entered this new stage of my writing.

Someone mentioned to me that this play feels like a newly written old Live Theatre play. Which may seem like an oxymoron but it's actually a huge compliment to me. Those plays they were referring to are the ones that inspired me to write.

Thank you to anyone who read this script or listened to me talk about it. I'd like to dedicate this play to my family. Though the McCarthy's struggle in this play to know how to love each other, you never do.

Nick Blakeley Ellis

Nick is originally from the North East and trained at The Bristol Old Vic Theatre School. He is an associate artist with Encounter and has recently been developing his own work during residencies with Camden People's Theatre and artsdepot.

Theatre credits include: *The Good Person of Szechwan* (Crucible/ETT/ Lyric Hammersmith); *The White Card* (Northern Stage); *The Claim* (Shoreditch Town Hall); *Twelfth Night* (Orange Tree Theatre); *I Heart Catherine Pistachio* (Soho Theatre/Yard Theatre); *Brideshead Revisited* (York Theatre Royal/UK Tour); *Hapgood* (Hampstead Theatre); *Comment Is Free* (Old Vic Theatre); *The Last of the De Mullins* (Jermyn St Theatre); *Hard Feelings* (Finborough Theatre); *The Sunshine Boys* (Savoy Theatre); *13*, *A Woman Killed With Kindness* (National Theatre); and *24 Hour Plays* (The Old Vic).

TV credits include: *Father Brown* (BBC); *Belgravia* (ITV); *Summer of Rockets* (BBC); *Theresa Vs Boris: How May Became PM* (BBC); *Beyond Reasonable Doubt* (CNN); *Doctors* (BBC); and *The Old Bailey* (BBC).

Film includes: *One Life* (See-Saw Films); *Northern Comfort* (Netop Films); *Goodbye Christopher Robin* (Fox Searchlight) and *Eyes and Prize* (Independent Film).

Jane Holman Evelyn

Theatre credits include: *Lush Life*, *Oh! What a Lovely War*, *Twelve Tales of Tyneside*, *Cabaret*, *Lenya* and *In Blackberry Time* (all for Live Theatre); *Tyne* (Live Theatre/Theatre Royal Newcastle); *Looking for Buddy* (Bolton Octagon/Live Theatre/Customs House); *Close the Coalhouse Door* (Northern Stage); *Beyond the End of the Road* (November Club and tour); *My Granny Is a Pirate* (New Writing North); *Maggie's End* and *Beamish Boy* (Gala Theatre Durham); *Sleeping Beauty* and *Dick Whittington* (Tyne Theatre); *Get Santa* (Northern Stage); *The Revengers* and *Cuddy's Miles* (Customs House South Shields).

Television credits include: *Vera*, *Inspector George Gently*, *Undercover*, and *The Dumping Ground* and feature films: *School for Seduction*, *Harrigan's Nick* and *Billy Elliot*.

Jane was singer, songwriter and guitarist for rock band JAZAWAKI and she has been musical director and arranger for a number of theatre and television productions. Jane is the singer/songwriter with the Questionnaires.

Amara Karan Ayeesha

Theatre credits include: *Bloody Difficult Women* (Wind of Change/Cahoots Theatre Company); *Much Ado About Nothing*, *The Taming of the Shrew*, *The Merchant of Venice*, *A Midsummer Night's Dream* (RSC).

Film credits include: *House of Spoils* (Amazon Studios); *T.I.M.* (Arthro Film); *The Death and Life of John F. Donovan* (Entertainment One); *Those Four Walls* (Malaika Films); *The Upside* (The Weinstein Company); *A Fantastic Fear of Everything* (Indomina Productions); *Jadoo* (Jadoo Films Ltd); *Jayden* (New Talent Productions/Malaika Entertainment); *All in Good Time* (Studio Canal); *Rafta Rafta* (Optimum); *The Task* (After Dark Productions); *St Trinian's* (Ealing Studios); *The Darjeeling Limited* (Fox Searchlight).

Television credits include: *Moonhaven* (AMC Studios); *Hope Street*, *The Beard*, *The Ambassadors*, *Doctor Who*, *The Good Housekeeping Guide* (BBC); *The Twilight Zone* (CBS); *Bancroft* (ITC Encore); *The Night Of* (HBO); *Lucky Man* – Seasons 1, 2 & 3 (Carnival Productions); *The Bill* (Talkback Thames); *Kidnap & Ransom* (Left Bank Productions); *Poirot – A Cat Among The Pigeons* (ITV Studios).

Jim Kitson David

Theatre credits include: *Red Ellen* (Nottingham Playhouse); *Wind in the Willows* (Derby Theatre); *Treasure Island* (Derby Theatre); *A Viking Christmas* – also MD (Queen's Hall Arts Centre); *Vanessa* – also Director (Purple Theatre); *The Grinning Man* (Trafalgar Studios); *Pitmen Painters* (New Vic Theatre); *The Grapes of Wrath* (Nottingham Playhouse/Royal & Derngate/West Yorkshire Playhouse); *Much Ado About Nothing* (Shakespeare's Globe); *The Drowned Man* (Punchdrunk/National Theatre); *Richard III*, *King John*, *Tyneside Tales* (Royal Shakespeare Company); *To Kill A Mockingbird* (Manchester Royal Exchange); *The Grapes of Wrath* (West Yorkshire Playhouse); *A Walk On Part: The Slow Fall of New Labour* (Soho Theatre); *What Happened is This* (Tron, Glasgow); *Noir*, *The Boy on the Swing*, *The*

Taxi Driver's Daughter, *13.1* (Live Theatre, Newcastle); *Cooking with Elvis*, *Office Party* (Hull Truck); *Son of Man*, *Animal Farm*, *Edmond*, *Glengarry Glen Ross* (Northern Stage); *Treasure Island*, *The Gift and the Glory* (Dukes, Lancaster); *Great Expectations* (Aberystwyth Arts Centre); *The New Tenant* (Hungarian State Theatre, Cluj, Romania).

Television credits include: *Dinosaur* (Two Brothers Pictures); *Clodagh* (Afternoon Picture); *The Red King* (UKTV/Quay Street Productions); *Land of Women* (Apple+); *King Gary* (Series 2); *Inspector George Gently* (Company Pictures for BBC); *Vera* (ITV Studios); *Emmerdale* (Yorkshire TV); *Joe Maddison's War* (Mammoth Productions for ITV1); *Tracy Beaker Returns* (CBBC); *Byker Grove* (Zenith Entertainment for BBC).

Beth Fletcher Morris Max

After recently graduating from BTEC Performing Arts at Newcastle College, Beth is thrilled to be back at Live Theatre to play the role of Max in *The Cold Buffet*.

Theatre credits include: Lord Brockhurst in *The Boy Friend* (Newcastle College); Bobo in *We Are The Best!* (Live Theatre); Dandini in *Cinderella* (Whitley Bay Pantomime Society) and Young Estella in *Great Expectations* (Tynemouth Priory Theatre).

They have also previously trained at Saturday Stage School Whitley Bay and were involved in productions there, as well as *Goldilocks and the Three Bears*, *Aladdin* and *Dick Whittington* with Whitley Bay Pantomime Society.

Creative & Production Team

Elijah Young Writer

Elijah Young is a North-East based playwright originally from Teesside. He received the Young Writer Residency Award for his play *Isolation* at The Customs House and was named by North East British Theatre Guide as Most Promising Newcomer 2019. He has also worked with several other theatres and companies in the region as a writer/dramaturg such as *NASA lie the Earth is flat No Curve* (Alphabetti Theatre); *Biscuit Tins* (Blowin' A Hooley Theatre) and *Remarkable Robin's Christmas Adventure* (Queens Hall Hexham, Alnwick Playhouse). His most recent work includes: *Worlds Apart, Am I Alone in This?*, *Father Unknown* (Northern Stage). *The Cold Buffet* was commissioned by Live Theatre during Elijah's time as an Associate Artist.

Jack McNamara Director

Jack has been Artistic Director and Joint CEO of Live Theatre in Newcastle since 2021. Productions for the company as director include: *We Are The Best*! and *One Off*. Previously he was Artistic Director of New Perspectives in Nottingham, where productions included the multiple award-winning *The Fishermen* (West End, Home Manchester, BBC Radio 3, British Council Showcase); *The Lovesong of Alfred J Hitchcock* (Off Broadway); The Boss of it All (Soho Theatre/Offie Nominated); *Darkness Darkness* (Nottingham Playhouse) and first national tours of plays by Athol Fugard and debbie tucker green among many others. Recent freelance work includes: *Shy* by Max Porter (Southbank Centre) starring Toby Jones and Ruth Wilson. He directed the epic audiobook *Voice of the Fire* by Alan Moore starring Maxine Peake, Mark Gatiss and Jason Williamson of Sleaford Mods.

Alison Ashton Designer

Alison gained a first class degree in theatre design and has since designed a wide range of productions for numerous theatre companies throughout the country. After learning her trade at the Birmingham Rep, RSC, Young Vic and Half Moon, London she was Associate Designer at the Royal & Derngate Northampton where one of her favourite designs was for the lavish restoration comedy *The Way of the World*. Since moving to Newcastle she has designed many productions for Open Clasp, Theatre sans Frontiers, Alphabetti and Kitchen Zoo.

Alison has created artwork and installations for Centrica and the Newcastle Building Society and since making the Storytelling Chair for Seven Stories has produced many more for schools, libraries, theatres and Durham Cathedral. In 2017 she worked alongside National Theatre director Tim Supple on *Freedom on the Tyne* a large scale community project which culminated in a performance on the Tyne Bridge.

Alison has designed several productions for Live Theatre including: *Love It If We Beat Them, Rendezvous*, *Turning Tales*, *The Savage*, *Harriet Martineau Dreams of Dancing* and *My Romantic History.*

Adam P. McCready Sound Designer/Composer

Adam is a sound designer, composer, producer, sound recordist, performer of Edgelands-Electronica and mentor.

Theatre credits include: *You Bury Me* (Paines Plough); *One Off* (Live Theatre, Newcastle); *Compositor E* (Omnibus Theatre); *71 Coltman Street*, *TWO, The Beauty Queen of Leenane, Abigail's Party* (Hull Truck); *Crongton Knights, Noughts and Crosses, Brighton Rock* (Pilot Theatre); *We Should Definitely Have More Dancing, The Jungle Book* (Oldham Coliseum); *The Cherry Orchard, Arcadia, A Skull in Connemara, Chicken Soup with Barley* (Nottingham Playhouse); *The Fishermen; trade; Maryland; The Great Almighty Gill* (New Perspectives).

Audio credits include: *Voice of the Fire* by Alan Moore (Audible); *The Fishermen* (BBC Radio 3, Naked Productions); *Letters of Constraint* (National Justice Museum); *The Black Dog, From Sad Shires* (Little Pixie Productions); *PlacePrints* (New Perspectives).

Installations: *Objects of Love and Hope & Fear* (Derby Museums); *Conflict & Chaos* (National Civil War Centre).

David Flynn Associate Sound Designer

David trained in Media Production before working in theatre, events and live music as a sound engineer and AV technician. He is currently Technical Manager for Live Theatre, one of the UK's leading new writing theatres renowned for producing and presenting new plays.

David is also a freelance sound designer. Sound design credits include: *Chop, Dissolve, Burn* (Alphabetti Theatre); *Educating Rita* (national tour/Theatre by the Lake/David Pugh); *One Off* (Live Theatre); *Clear White Light, My Romantic History*, Olivier Nominated *The Red Lion* (Live Theatre/Trafalgar Studio's London); *The Savage, Harriet Martineau Dreams of Dancing, Flying into Daylight, Wet House* (Live Theatre/Hull Truck/Soho Theatre); *Cooking with Elvis, Faith and Cold Reading, A Walk on Part* (Live Theatre/Soho Theatre/Arts Theatre London); *A Northern Odyssey* (Live Theatre).

Drummond Orr Lighting Designer/Production Manager

Drummond has over 40 years' experience as a theatre electrician, technical manager, lighting designer and production manager. In that time, he has toured nationally and internationally, and has worked in both touring and production theatre.

Lighting design credits include: *Love It If We Beat Them* (Live Theatre), *One Off* (Live Theatre); *The Red Lion* (Live Theatre/Trafalgar Studios); *My Romantic History, The Savage, Cooking with Elvis* and *Wet House* (Live Theatre/Hull Truck/Soho Theatre); *Tyne, The Prize, Nativities, Two Pints* and *A Walk on Part* (Live Theatre/Soho Theatre/Arts Theatre); *Blackbird* (Market Theatre, Johannesburg); *The Girl in the Yellow Dress* (Market Theatre, Johannesburg/Grahamstown Festival/Baxter Theatre, Cape Town/Citizens, Glasgow); *Educating Rita* (Theatre by the Lake/David Pugh and UK tour).

About Live Theatre

'One of the most fertile crucibles of new writing' **The Guardian**

Live Theatre occupies a unique place as one of the country's only dedicated new writing buildings outside of London. Across its fifty-year history it has launched the careers of many of today's leading theatre figures and continues to develop and platform the artists of tomorrow, from playwrights to local school children. Deeply connected to its region and unafraid to confront the most pressing issues of our time, Live Theatre brings ambitious regional artists and adventurous local audiences into vivid contact.

'Live Theatre has supported generation after generation of new writers, actors and theatre artists.' **Lee Hall, Playwright**

To learn more about Live Theatre and get involved see www.live.org.uk

Best Friends

Noreen Bates
Jim Beirne
Michael and Pat Brown
George Caulkin
Sue and Simon Clugston
Helen Coyne
Christine Elton
Chris Foy
Robson Green
Brenna Hobson
John Jordan

Graham Maddick
Elaine Orrick
Paul Shevlin
Margaret and John Shipley
Shelagh Stephenson
Sting
Alan Tailford
David Walton
Sue Wilson
Lucy Winskell

Good Friends

Vincent Allen
John Appleton
Jeff and Susan Brown
Robin Cantrill-Fenwick

Alec Collerton
Ron Cook
Angela Coulthard and David Wright
Joe Douglas

Ann Gittins
Eileen Jones
John Mason
Rhys McKinnell
David Nellist
Chris Connell and Lucy Nichol
Linda Norris
Michelle Percy
Pat Ritchie

Martin Saunders
Phil Skingley
Susan and Mike Stewart
John Stokel-Walker
John Tomaney
Angela Walton
K F Walton
Mary and Steve Wootten

Friends

Pat Allcorn
Sharon Austin
Norma Banfi
Bex Bowsher
Lawrence Bryson
Rob Chapman
Sally-Anne Cooper
Angela Cooper
Judy Cowgill
Glynis Downie
Suky Drummond
Keith Elliott
Sue Emmas
Robert Fairfax
David Fenwick
Carolyn Ford
Joanna Foster
John Graham
Julie Grant
Moira Gray
Dorothy Hair
Gael Henry
Ruth and Robert Heyman
Gillian Hitchenes
Wendy Holland
Irene Hudson
Beverley Jewitt
Richard Kain

Nicole Kavanagh-Stubbs
John Loughlin
Gen Lowes
Stephanie Malyon
Sarah Marshall
Michael McBride
Ian Mowbray
Linda Moss
Stephanie O'Connor
Jean Ollerton
Clare Overton
Jonathan Pye
David Robertson
Jo Robinson
Julian Rogan
Jean Scott
Jill Scrimshaw
Alan and Rosalind Share
Monica Shaw
Jo Shepherd
Ian and Christine Shepherdson
Tracey Sinclair
Brent Taylorson
Don Tennet
Robert Vardill
Sandra Wake
Sue Ward
Keith Williamson

PLUS THOSE WHO CHOOSE TO REMAIN ANONYMOUS

Live Theatre Staff

Executive Director/Joint Chief Executive **Jacqui Kell**
Artistic Director/Joint Chief Executive **Jack McNamara**
PA to Joint Chief Executives **Alex Readman**

Creative Programme
New Work Producer **JD Stewart**
Projects Producer **John Dawson**
Associate Artists **gobscure**
Kemi-Bo Jacobs

Children and Young People
CYPP Leader **Helen Green**
Senior Creative Associate CYPP **Paul James**
CYPP Administrator **Amy Foley**
Creative Lead Live Tales **Becky Morris**

Technical Production
Production Manager **Drummond Orr**
Technical and Digital Manager **David Flynn**
Technician **Taylor Howie**
Estates and Maintenance Assistant **Ken Evans**

Operations and Finance
Finance and Operations Manager **Antony Robertson**
Finance and Payroll Officer **Catherine Moody**
Fundraising and Development Manager **Alison Nicholson**

Marketing and Communications
Marketing and Communications Manager **Lisa Campbell**
Marketing and Communications Manager **Michele McCallion**

Customer Services and Box Office
Customer Services and Estate Manager **Ben Young**
Duty Manager **Michael Davies**
Duty Manager and Bar Supervisor **Alicia Meehan**
Duty Manager and Bar Supervisor **Arthur Roberts**
Duty Manager and Bar Supervisor **Patryoja Nowacka**
Bar Supervisor **Fay Carrington**
Bar Supervisor **Jake Wilson Craw**
Customer Service Assistant **Caitlin Fairlamb**
Customer Service Assistant **Brennan Flanders**
Customer Service Assistant **Elspeth Frith**
Customer Service Assistant **Sarah Matthews**
Customer Service Assistant **Kathryn Watt**
Customer Service Assistant **Bridget Marumo**
Customer Service Assistant **Joel Houghton**
Customer Service Assistant **Lukas Gabryseh**
Customer Service Assistant **Alicja Gadomski**
Customer Service Assistant **Hannah Guthrie**
Box Office Assistant **Steven Blackshaw**
Box Office Assistant **Daniel Ball**
Box Office Assistant **Ruby Taylor**

Box Office Assistant	**Hannah Sparkes**
Box Office Assistant	**Jasper Wilding**
Box Office Assistant	**Joseph Duffy**

Housekeeping

Housekeeping	**Angela Salem**
Housekeeping	**Jean Kent**
Housekeeping	**Lydia Igbinosa**
Housekeeping	**Camille Vitorino-Itoua**

The Cold Buffet

Characters

Ellis, *late twenties/early thirties. He/Him.*
Evelyn, *seventies. She/Her.*
David, *fifties. He/Him.*
Ayeesha, *mid thirties/forties. She/Her.*
Max, *late teens/early twenties. AFAB. They/Them.*

Setting

North East of England. The play happens over the course of five years. It takes place in an unused function room where the cold buffet is displayed in the centre.

Inspired by Dorman Long United Athletic Club, Middlesbrough.

There is a door that leads to the main bar and another door that leads outside to a smoking area.

Notes

The transitions between the acts are up to the artistic vision of the director.

(/) indicates an interruption

(Beat.) indicates pauses or suggests the rhythm of how the text is delivered.

(A moment.) indicates an emotional beat, a pause that feels slightly too long.

Act One

The Wake. Mid 2017

David *enters in a black suit holding the microphone.*

David   Is this working . . . Yeah? So you can hear us? Right. Cheers. Thanks for coming. Our dad would be . . . yeah, you know, with the turnout and that. I've been asked to come up and share this on behalf of everyone here . . .

He gets out a piece of paper and reads.

Erm. Paul . . . yeah . . . Paul is in the DJ booth today and does take requests, karaoke starts in an hour, there's a deal on at the bar three bottles of Woodpecker for five pound, the downstairs ladies is out of order and the buffet is now open and through the door on the right.

He folds the paper and puts it back in his pocket.

Cheers. Have a good one.

An unused function room. A few chairs, an empty bar. The buffet is the centrepiece.

Evelyn *enters in black.*

She takes a moment to allow herself to be emotional before composing herself.

She approaches the buffet. She takes out her cigarettes and goes to light up.

David *enters.*

David   You can't smoke in here.

Evelyn   I can do what I like.

Evelyn *tuts and reluctantly puts the cigarettes away.*

People have barely touched it.

David You what?

Evelyn This.

David Oh.

Evelyn No one's having a nice time.

David I think I'm enjoying myself.

Evelyn Right.

David Did you expect them to?

Evelyn Obviously. Everyone kept going on about there being enough food and yet . . .

David Maybe they're not hungry.

Evelyn Well, I bloody paid for it so they better hurry up and get an appetite.

David Why don't you eat something?

Evelyn No.

David Why?

Evelyn I'm not hungry. Why are you lurking, David?

David What?

Evelyn You're lurking, hovering. You're following me.

David I'm checking in on you.

Evelyn You don't need to.

David It was nice. The service.

Evelyn Was it?

David It was.

Pause.

Mam.

Evelyn What?

David   Did you . . .

Evelyn   What?

David   Did you fall asleep?

Evelyn   What?

David   Did you fall asleep?

Evelyn   Did I fall asleep?

David   Your eyes were closed, Mam.

Evelyn   Did I fall asleep at my own husband's funeral, David?

David   I'm not saying you did.

Evelyn   I was listening.

David   Right.

Evelyn   I was. You were laughing.

David   You saw that?

Evelyn   I wasn't the only one. It was embarrassing. Poor Father Michael.

David   Oh haway. He's a horrendous singer.

Evelyn   Jesus loves his voice.

David   Oh he would, wouldn't he.

Evelyn   Is Ellis still here?

David   Yeah.

Evelyn   Nice of him to come. I was surprised.

David   He comes when I ask him.

Evelyn   Beg him more like.

David   He wouldn't have missed Dad's funeral.

Evelyn   I noticed he didn't take communion in the church.

David   Does that matter?

Evelyn   People notice these things. He doesn't respect you.

David   He does.

Evelyn   And that's your fault.

David   Alright.

Evelyn   I'm not wrong. You were never like that. Especially not to your father.

David   I'm not Dad.

Evelyn   Don't we know that.

David   Don't be . . .

Evelyn   What? What?

David   I know your husband's just died.

Evelyn   I don't know what you're on about, David. I'm having a lovely time. I wish everyone else was. These chicken skewers are supposed to be quite good. Here, have one.

She offers the plate.

David   Can you do something for me?

Evelyn   Here.

She offers again.

David   Mam.

Evelyn   Go on.

David   Can you be nice to Ayeesha?

Evelyn   I'm very nice.

David   Mother.

Evelyn   I'm nice enough.

David   Extra nice would be helpful. You ignored her earlier.

Evelyn   Look, I've only met her a handful of times /

David   And what? You don't trust her?

Evelyn   I trust my gut.

David   Most illnesses start in the gut.

Evelyn   What are you suggesting about my gut health?

David   I'd like you to try a bit more.

Evelyn   Why did you bring her?

David   Don't ask daft questions.

Evelyn   The amount of looks off everyone in the church when she came in with you. It's uncomfortable.

David   What's that supposed to mean?

Evelyn   Not like that. I never said like that.

David   Well?

Evelyn   She's just so young.

David   You've said.

Evelyn   It was distracting people. And when someone your age has someone young, who looks like her on your arm /

David   Mother /

Evelyn   All dolled up is what I meant, before you start. People talk.

David   I don't care what people think.

Evelyn   Well maybe you should. It just gives off the wrong impression, David. People would make less of a fuss if you walked in with a proddy dog.

David   People need to get a life.

Pause.

Evelyn   She's just a lot.

David   And you're a walk in the park, aren't you?

Evelyn   On a summer's day when the grass is freshly cut. David, she cried more than I bloody did in the service. It's a bit . . .

David   She's an emotional person.

Evelyn   I gathered.

David   Can you just try? She tries with you. She's family now.

Evelyn   Is she?

David   I say she is.

A moment.

Did she turn up then?

Evelyn   Who?

David   You know?

Evelyn   Oh.

David   I couldn't spot her in the church or the crem /

Evelyn   I didn't see her.

David   I knew you were worried about it, is all.

Evelyn   I wasn't worried, why would you say that?

David   Okay, so she didn't /

Evelyn   I didn't see her, David.

David   Right.

A moment. **David** *goes to leave.*

Evelyn   It's a shame you didn't speak.

David   What?

Evelyn   In the service. At the church or the crematorium.

David   I just thanked everyone twenty minutes ago.

Evelyn   That's not what I meant.

Beat.

He would've wanted you to speak. To say something.
Anything.

David   Well, I didn't want to.

Evelyn   Your brother spoke.

David   And?

Evelyn   It just would've been nice since I asked.

David   I didn't want to.

Evelyn *tuts.*

David   What?

Evelyn   You do things to intentionally upset me.

Ayeesha *enters with a tray covered in tin foil.*

Ayeesha   Ooh sorry. I wasn't interrupting, was I?

David   No, you weren't.

Ayeesha   Evelyn.

Evelyn   Yes?

Ayeesha   Come here.

Ayeesha *awkwardly hugs* **Evelyn**.

Ayeesha   God, you'll set me off again. You alright, darling?

David   I'm fine.

Ayeesha   He was a really lovely man.

Evelyn   Thank you.

Ayeesha *kisses* **David** *on the cheek.*

Ayeesha   We brought some sandwiches, Evelyn. I'll just pop them here. I made quite a few cos you always worry there's not going to be enough at these things.

Evelyn   More food for no one to eat.

Ayeesha   I ate a sausage roll earlier.

Evelyn   You're a saint.

Ayeesha   You look lovely by the way, Evelyn. Really, really lovely.

Evelyn   Thank you.

Ayeesha   You should wear black more often.

Evelyn   No.

Ayeesha   We should get Max to take a photo.

Evelyn   Of what?

Ayeesha   Of us. That would be nice, wouldn't it?

Evelyn   Right.

Ayeesha   The service was wonderful.

Evelyn   Yep.

Ayeesha   Such a traditional funeral. There's something so elegant about a traditional funeral. Do you know what I mean?

Evelyn *nods*.

Ayeesha   Father Michael's voice is so soothing I almost fell asleep too.

Evelyn   You what?

Ayeesha   David said you fell asleep.

Evelyn   I didn't fall asleep. Tell him I didn't.

Ayeesha   Apparently she didn't.

David Yep.

Evelyn Martin's tribute was beautiful, wasn't it?

Ayeesha Oh I laughed and cried through the whole thing. 'John died so that he didn't have to see Theresa May win the general election.' Brilliant.

Ayeesha *laughs.*

David He hated her.

Ayeesha And that one line really stuck with me. No song for the broken-hearted, no silent prayer for faith-departed. Something like that. Is that from the Bible?

David It's Bon Jovi.

Ayeesha Oh.

Max *enters.*

Max I don't want to take photos anymore.

Ayeesha Why?

Max Everyone keeps crying.

David It is a funeral.

Max Grandad's sister just told me off.

Evelyn Oh don't listen to her, a photo of Frances would break your bloody camera.

David Mam.

Evelyn What? She's ugly.

David Don't tell that to her, Max.

Max I'm not an idiot.

Ayeesha Max, take a photo of me and your grandma? We're not crying.

Max Can I grab a plate first?

Evelyn   Let the poor bairn eat something.

Max   Grandma, did you actually fall asleep?

Evelyn   Right, I'm paying you twenty quid to take photos. Hurry up.

David   Here, have a drumstick. They're not that bad.

Evelyn   Nothing is bad.

David   The quiche is sub par. The chicken is alright.

Ayeesha   Max is actually vegan.

Max   No I'm not.

Ayeesha   Oh right.

Evelyn   Well, have something.

Max   Why?

Evelyn   Cos I paid for it.

Max   But it's all cold.

Evelyn   And?

Ayeesha   Have a sandwich, Max.

Max   I don't like corned beef.

Ayeesha   Egg and cress?

Max   Ew.

Evelyn   There's ham.

Max   Is it buttered?

David   Most of them are.

Max   I don't like butter.

Ayeesha   There's peanut butter.

Evelyn   Just eat something.

Max   Alright.

Ayeesha   Max. How are you feeling, darling?

Max   Okay.

Ayeesha   Your grandad loved you, you know.

Max   Uncle David, can you buy me a pint?

David   How old are you?

Max *bites into the sandwich.*

Max   Eighteen.

David   Yeah, right.

Max   There's butter on this.

They spit it out.

Ayeesha   What?

Max   There's butter on the peanut butter sandwiches.

Ayeesha   Oh. Whoops.

Max   Who puts butter on butter?

Ayeesha   I just buttered all the bread.

Max   Butter on butter?

Ayeesha   It's just butter.

Max   Why would you do that?

David   Watch your manners, Max.

Max   But it's rank.

David   Oi, Max! Ayeesha was kind enough to make those sandwiches. Say sorry.

Evelyn   David.

David   What?

Evelyn   Don't start telling off kids that aren't yours.

David   Max is being rude.

Evelyn   I'm just saying, remember last time you told Max off in front of Martin.

David   I don't care. Max.

Max   Sorry.

Evelyn   It's not your fault, love.

David   You've drank that a bit fast, haven't you Mam?

Evelyn   Are you going to tell me off as well?

David   Maybe slow down a bit.

Evelyn   Slow down?

David   Yeah.

Evelyn   Why don't you go find your own son if you fancy telling someone off, instead of bothering everyone else?

Ellis *enters wiping his shirt, not noticing* **Max**.

Ellis   For fuck's sake.

David   Ellis.

Ellis   Sorry, yes I know, sorry. Uncle Martin spilt Foster's on my shirt. Nice of him to turn up plastered to his own dad's funeral.

David   Son.

A moment. He realises.

Ellis   Oh . . . erm. Megan.

Ayeesha   It's Max now.

Ellis   Shit. Sorry. Yeah. Max.

Max *smiles awkwardly.*

Ellis   Your dad was saying . . . you know, it doesn't matter really he's harmless /

David   Let's go buy you a drink, Max-a-million.

Max   Really?

David   What's your favourite flavour of J2O?

Max   Get lost.

David   What? You don't even like the one with the sprinkles of glitter?

Max   No, that's you.

David   Haway, I'll get you a beer.

Max   Pint?

David   A half.

Max *exits.*

Evelyn (*referencing her empty glass*)   Another, David. If you don't mind.

Beat.

David *exits.*

Evelyn   Did you think Max needed to hear that, Ellis?

Ellis   I didn't know.

Evelyn *exits.*

Ayeesha   It's fine. I'm sure she . . . sorry. They. I'm sure they'll forget about it.

Beat.

Are we hugging?

Ellis   Yeah. Sure.

Ayeesha *hugs him for a little too long.*

Ayeesha   It's so nice to properly meet you in the flesh, darling. I know it's obviously not the most ideal place for us to meet but you know at least it's got us together. I am so sorry about your grandad. How are you feeling?

Ellis   I'm okay.

Ayeesha   He loved you, you know.

Ellis   Thanks.

Ayeesha   I was thinking, Ellis, you should really try to spend some time with Max. There's no one else their age in the family.

Ellis   Isn't Max a teenager?

Ayeesha   Well, the closest in age.

Ellis   Ah. Is it cos I'm a homosexual?

Ayeesha   I mean I think you could be a good gay role model for them. I think they're gay.

Ellis   Max and my dad get along well.

Ayeesha   Thick as thieves, those two.

Ellis   So where did you two meet?

Ayeesha   Has he not said?

Ellis   No.

Ayeesha   Oh, it's a bit embarrassing.

Ellis   Is it?

Ayeesha   We met through his work.

Ellis   As in . . .

Ayeesha   He was my driving instructor. Oh, you probably think it's so silly. I'm so old.

Ellis   I wasn't thinking that.

Ayeesha   I put it off for years but it's better for work and I got sick of paying for trains to see family. You'll know all about that.

Ellis   Yep.

Ayeesha Nothing happened until I passed. It was all . . . appropriate.

Ellis And did you?

Ayeesha Second attempt. Only a couple of minors. He's a good teacher. Bet he taught you early.

Ellis I was never interested.

Ayeesha He was right. You don't really look like him.

Ellis He said that?

Ayeesha Do you think you look more like your mum?

Ellis I don't know.

Ayeesha You're handsome though. You get that from your dad.

Ellis Thanks.

Ayeesha You know, there's this TA at the school I work at. We're good friends. He's so lovely, from around here. You probably know each other.

Ellis Oh, I have a boyfriend.

Ayeesha Oh?

Ellis Yeah?

Ayeesha Oh. Is that a new thing?

Ellis No, no. Two years.

Ayeesha Oh right.

Ellis Did my dad not mention it?

Ayeesha Oh yeah, yeah. He probably did. He definitely did.

Pause.

Ayeesha Whereabouts in London are you? My parents are in Wood Green.

Ellis   We're in Hackney.

Ayeesha   Oh my God. I've just realised you will have been there, won't you? For the London Bridge attacks over the weekend.

Ellis   And Borough Market.

Ayeesha   God.

Ellis   I work in the city centre so it was pretty . . .

Ayeesha   Terrifying. I couldn't stop ringing my mum. First Manchester and now . . . it's a scary time.

Ellis   It is.

Ayeesha   Bet you're glad to be home.

Ellis   Yeah.

Evelyn *enters with a glass of wine, she begins to plate up food.*

Ayeesha   I was sorry to miss you at Christmas.

Ellis   I'm normally only there for the day. I was working a lot.

Ayeesha   So are you still dancing?

Ellis   When I get the jobs.

Evelyn   He works in recruitment, don't you?

Ellis   Yep.

Evelyn   Whatever that means.

Ayeesha   I thought you were a barista.

Ellis   Not anymore.

Ayeesha   You should be a choreographer. Or go on *Strictly*. Shouldn't he go on *Strictly*, Evelyn?

Evelyn   I think you should do what Max is doing.

Ellis   And what's that?

Evelyn   University. Applying to study science.

Ellis   I went to university.

Ayeesha   Did you?

Evelyn   I thought it was a dance school.

Ellis   I still got a degree, Grandma.

Evelyn   I used to send him money to help out.

Ayeesha   That's kind.

Evelyn   It all paid off, didn't it?

Ayeesha   Bet it was scary moving to London on your own.

Ellis   I lived off pasta and Lucozade.

Evelyn   He was so slim back then.

Ellis   She means I was starving.

Evelyn   You make up for it now. He spends a lot of time by the buffet table.

Ellis   Erm.

Evelyn   There's nothing wrong with it. But you need discipline to do well in the industry though. You've lost some of that.

Ayeesha   You do still dance though, don't you? I heard you did that advert last year.

Ellis   I did.

Evelyn   I warned him it wasn't a stable career. But he wouldn't listen, Ayeesha. He's stubborn like his dad. You'll know that.

David *enters*.

David   Aunty June's heading off.

Evelyn   She loves to leave early.

David   Mam, she has osteoporosis.

Evelyn   Alright, stop shouting at me. Let me sort her a doggie bag.

Ellis   Don't forget to pop in the toy with a slice of cake.

Evelyn *ignores this.*

Ayeesha   Do you need help getting up?

Evelyn   You're alright, Ayeesha.

Evelyn *picks up a napkin and fills it with bits of food.*

Ayeesha   I'll come say goodbye.

Evelyn   If at least seventy-five per cent of this food hasn't gone by the end of tonight, I might just throw myself off a roof.

Evelyn *and* **Ayeesha** *exit.*

A moment.

Ellis (*aside*)   Do you need help getting up?

Ellis *scans the cold buffet. He begins to put food on the plate.*

Max *enters unnoticed.*

Max   There's butter in that.

Ellis   Jesus!

Ellis *spills his plate on the floor.*

Ellis   Well, that's a waste of a Scotch egg.

Max   Five second rule?

Ellis   I'd rather not. These carpets. Riddled with lager, piss and Catholic guilt.

Ellis *picks up the food and leaves the plate on the side.*

Ellis   My dad buy you a drink?

Max   Strongbow.

Ellis He's getting soft.

Max How?

Ellis He'd never buy me a drink at fifteen.

Max I'm seventeen.

Ellis Oh. Sorry.

Beat.

Ellis How's things, Max?

Max Fine.

Ellis College going okay?

Max Yeah.

Ellis Cool cool cool cool cool.

Beat.

What's with the camera?

Max Grandma asked me to take photos.

Ellis At a funeral? Bit weird.

Max Ayeesha said I should get a photo of us.

Ellis Did she?

Beat.

Did you say the peanut butter sandwich has butter in it?

Max Yep.

Ellis May I ask why?

Max I don't know. Ayeesha made them.

Beat.

Do you like her then?

Ellis Why?

Max   Curious.

Ellis   Do you like her?

Max   I think she's sound when she's not buttering peanut butter sandwiches. Do you like her?

Ellis   I barely know her.

Max   Isn't she like your age?

Ellis   About seven years older.

Max   Oh. Not too bad.

Ellis   When my dad was your age, she wasn't alive yet.

Max   Oh. Yikes. Sort of bad.

Ellis   Yeah. I don't think it's bad, it's just . . . it's interesting.

Beat.

She thinks I'm a good gay role model for you.

Max   She said that?

Ellis   Something like that.

Max   That's hilarious.

A moment.

Ellis   What do you mean?

Max   That's so funny.

Ellis   So you don't think I'd be a good gay role model?

Max   Do you think you're a good gay role model?

Ellis   I think I could be.

Max   Sure.

Ellis   Excuse me, I was gay in this family before it became 'fascinating'.

Max   I'm actually pan.

Beat.

Ellis   Aren't you supposed to be all shy and mysterious?

Max   Eh?

Ellis   That's always been my perception.

Max   What?

Ellis   I thought you were quiet.

Max   That's cos you never talk to me.

No response.

Ellis   Sorry, you know, erm. I'm sorry. What I said about your dad earlier, it was /

Max   Everything you said was true. My mam doesn't like me coming to these sorts of things.

Ellis   Why?

Max   Cos they get ugly. But you know, I wanted to be here.

Beat.

When did you last see him?

Ellis   Grandad?

Max *nods.*

Ellis   Christmas. You?

Max   About two weeks ago.

Beat.

Did you cry at the funeral?

Ellis   Yeah.

Max   I didn't. It doesn't feel like he's dead.

David *and* **Evelyn** *burst in.*

David   Get in there.

Evelyn   Don't tell me to get anywhere.

David   And you said I was embarrassing for laughing in church.

Evelyn   I'm not having Duncan or Frances tell me where or when we can scatter the ashes of my husband.

David   He was their brother, Mam.

Evelyn   And have they acted like it? Didn't speak to him for years. Only became interested when he was dead and we all know why.

David   You need to calm down.

Ayeesha *enters.*

Ayeesha   What's going on?

Evelyn   Oh, don't you start.

David   Give us a second, love.

Evelyn   I'll have more than a second if you don't mind.

David   Kids, get out.

They don't.

Ayeesha   Duncan seems upset.

David   I'm sorting it.

Evelyn   This kind of stuff has got nothing to do with you, sweetheart.

Ayeesha   Sorry?

Evelyn   You don't need to be in here, it's a family matter. Get her out, David.

Ayeesha   I'm just trying to help. Why don't we /

Evelyn   / Blood's thicker than water.

David   That's enough! You don't talk to her like that.

A moment.

Evelyn Duncan's not taking him to Ireland. They moved when he was seven and he's never bloody been back. He didn't care about it.

Max Where's Grandad going?

Evelyn Nowhere love, he's staying here.

David He just wants Dad with the rest of his family.

Evelyn So do I.

David It's important to him.

Evelyn I don't really care what he wants to be honest, David. I don't know why you're coming to his defence.

David It's not that big of a deal. Why can't we just divi the ashes up so everyone gets some? So it's fair.

Evelyn 'Divi the ashes up.' He's not a bloody sheet cake.

David Most of it isn't even him.

Evelyn Even more reason to keep all of him in one place then.

David Well, I want some.

Evelyn You what?

David I want to keep some of the ashes. Is that alright?

Evelyn Didn't think you would.

David Well, I do.

Max I want some.

Ellis Really?

Max Yeah. Why not? I'll have a half a bag, Grandma, not too much though.

Ellis Jesus Christ.

David   Ellis, do you want some of your grandad?

Ellis   Well, when you put it like that . . .

David   You don't have to decide now, son.

Evelyn   I don't get the little shoebox until tomorrow.

Ellis   I think I'm alright.

Max   Shoe box?

Evelyn   Well, it looks like one. It's very anticlimactic.

Max   Do the bones survive? Or is it all just crumbly bits?

Ellis   Okay. Can we stop? I'm starting to feel /

Ayeesha   Are you okay?

Max   Is it the butter on butter?

Ellis   If everyone stopped talking about my grandad's crumbly bits that would be great.

Evelyn   Happy to. He stays with the family.

David   It's a bit selfish though, Mam.

Evelyn   I think with all I've gone through I have a right to be a little bit selfish.

Ayeesha   Come on now, this is not what today's about.

Evelyn   I actually couldn't disagree more.

David   You forget why our dad and Duncan barely spoke.

Evelyn   I remember plenty.

David   You remember what you want. But we both know Dad pushed him away /

Evelyn   He did not /

David   And I'm not going to lie, I'm a bit sick of you talking about him like he was a saint.

Evelyn   I beg your pardon.

David   He could be a nasty piece of work, Mam, you know /

Evelyn   No, no, no. I'm not having this.

Evelyn *storms off back through to the main bar.*

David   I'm not wrong though. People forget. Just cos he's now dead doesn't mean /

Ayeesha   Okay, okay.

Ellis   Come on, Max.

Ellis *exits and* **Max** *follows.*

David   I know she can be bad sometimes but bloody hell.

Ayeesha   Let's just /

David   And it's funny really, she of all people knew what he was like. But you know, loyal to her own detriment and all that. That's the Catholic in her. Nana was the same. Rewriting history so they can sleep at night. Sick of it.

Ayeesha   I know.

David   None of us know how to deal with things. That's why our Martin's pissed off his face. He's an absolute mess.

Ayeesha   Come here.

Ayeesha *gives him a hug.*

Ayeesha   It's like hugging a brick wall. You need to calm down.

David   Easier said than done.

Ayeesha   You just need to take your mind of it.

David   Have any ideas?

Ayeesha   The karaoke will be on soon.

David   Oh Margaret will be hogging that. She'll sing 'Hopelessly Devoted To You' several times sporadically throughout the afternoon.

They laugh.

You think I'm joking.

Ayeesha   Will you sing with me?

David   What would you want to sing?

Ayeesha   What would you want to sing? If you say 'Five Hundred Miles', I refuse.

David   Oh come on. It's a crowd pleaser.

Ayeesha   Honestly, you'll never see me again.

David   Isn't that a song?

Ayeesha   'Cry For You' by September.

David   Eee. You're like a pub quiz on legs. You wouldn't leave me.

Ayeesha   Wouldn't I?

David   Nah. You're too lazy.

Ayeesha   Shut up you.

They kiss.

She doesn't like me.

David   Who?

Ayeesha   Who do you think?

David   My mother?

Ayeesha   She doesn't even try to hide it.

Beat.

David   How she is with you is what she's like with everyone.

I'm the person she doesn't like today.

Ayeesha   Why?

David   Cos I didn't speak at the service, did I? And she'll hold that against me. One of my mother's impressive talents is how much she can hold a grudge.

Ayeesha   Why didn't you?

David   Cos I didn't fancy it.

Ayeesha   Why?

David   Cos I just didn't. Surely that should be enough.

Ayeesha   Alright, alright. God, you're tense.

David   It'll be all the pressure put on my shoulders from my father.

Ayeesha   Is that what this is, David?

David   No, I mean I'm in pain from carrying the coffin, man. Martin was half cut so I was practically carrying it myself.

They laugh.

See. I carried the coffin like she asked but she'll not care about that. If I've done something wrong it's all she'll focus on.

Beat.

Me and our dad . . . It wasn't easy.

Ayeesha   Is it the same with you and Ellis?

David   Oh no. Me and Ellis are totally different.

Ayeesha   Do you think Ellis likes me?

David   Hard to tell.

Ayeesha   Why?

David   It's a bit of strange day to meet his dad's girlfriend.

Ayeesha   Partner.

David   What?

Ayeesha   Girlfriend sounds young.

David   You are so young.

Ayeesha   Do you talk to him about me?

David   Who?

Ayeesha   Ellis.

David   Erm, not really.

Ayeesha   Why?

David   You know we don't talk a lot.

Ayeesha   You do sometimes.

David   Rarely.

Ayeesha   And do I come up?

David   Yeah.

Ayeesha   And what do you say?

David   I say that you're lovely. Most of the time.

Ayeesha   And?

David   I say you're gorgeous.

Ayeesha   No you don't.

David   It's the truth.

They kiss as **Ellis** *enters.*

Ellis   Oop. Sorry.

David   Oh. Hiya son.

A moment of awkwardness.

Ellis   Should I . . .

Ayeesha   Oh no, you stay, darling.

Ayeesha *springs into action and starts plating up some food.*

I've barely had any of this spread. Let me just grab a few bits and I'll let you two catch up, ey?

Ayeesha *exits.*

A moment.

David   You alright then, son?

Ellis   Yeah.

Pause.

David   Come on then. You know what, I'm going to say. Anything you need to tell me?

Ellis   Not really.

David   Need any money?

Ellis   No.

David   Done your tax return?

Ellis   Yes.

David   Done anything illegal?

Ellis   Okay, HMRC. I'm all good.

David   Good.

Pause.

Ellis   Ayeesha is nice.

David   Yeah?

Ellis   Very erm . . . yeah, she's nice.

David   Right.

Ellis   Did she know Grandad?

David   Not really.

Ellis   Oh. I was surprised you brought her to be honest.

David   Why?

Beat.

We've been together for a while, Ellis.

Pause.

She wants me to propose.

Ellis   What?

David   Ayeesha.

Ellis   Wow.

David   What? Do you think I should?

Ellis   You really pick your moments, Dad.

David   What do you mean?

Ellis   I've come home because my grandad has just died.

David   I know that but /

Ellis   And you're picking now to tell me /

David   Ellis.

Ellis   Do you want my blessing or something?

David   No.

Ellis   Why are you telling me?

David   Why wouldn't I?

Ellis   But like today? Right now?

David   I don't when the next time I'm going to see you. You're never here.

Ellis   You can ring me.

David   You don't pick up the phone.

Ellis   I do sometimes.

David   You don't. People think you don't care, you know.

Ellis   Jesus. Dad, can we not?

David I'm just being honest. You show up when you want. Barely talk to anyone. Leave as soon as you can.

Ellis Maybe there's a reason for that.

David What's that supposed to me?

Ellis I can't wait to mysteriously not appear in any of the photos from today when Grandma makes an album.

David Don't you think that's you being a little paranoid?

Ellis You know what Uncle Martin said to me? Before he ruined my shirt? I wasn't asked to carry the coffin cos that's a job for the men.

David He said a load of shite to me, he's off his face.

Ellis Yet it's all on me. What am I doing? What can I do to show I care? How often can I visit? Cos you know, everyone comes to visit me, don't they?

David Son, come on now. You live in London.

Ellis I know. It's far away and expensive. Which is convenient. But somehow I make it here just fine on minimum wage.

David I've come down.

Ellis I graduated seven years ago, Dad and you haven't visited since. But that's a whole thing so I'm not going to even /

David Why don't you want to be here?

Ellis I'm not saying that /

David Did you not want to be here today?

Ellis I obviously wanted to be here. That's why I'm here. For you. And for me.

Beat.

I don't want to fight. You just buried your dad.

David   Cremated.

Ellis   Alright, smart arse.

Beat.

I wouldn't have started dancing if it wasn't for him.

David   He'd brag about you, you know. That it all came from him.

Ellis   Probably did. You can't dance for shit.

David   I get by.

Beat.

Ellis   Congrats by the way.

David   Huh?

Ellis   On the proposal.

David   Oh. I'm not going to propose.

Ellis   Why?

David   I don't want to get married again. Just forget I mentioned it.

Beat.

Ellis   Dad, are you alright?

David   Yeah. No. I'm . . . I'm fine. It's just all been very weird, you know with it being so sudden and that.

Ellis   Yeah.

David   I was erm . . . I was the one who found him so . . .

Ellis   Oh. Grandma wasn't there?

David   She was at church and he'd been feeling under the weather so she asked me to pop round and . . . yeah. Don't tell her I told you that. She feels guilty enough.

Ellis   God.

Beat.

Ellis   You know with today . . . Did she invite Aunty Jacqui /

David   No. And do not mention her either.

Beat.

Max *enters and takes a photo with flash.*

Ellis   What are you doing?

Max   Ayeesha said to get a photo of you two.

Ellis   Does that need to be right now?

Ayeesha *enters.*

David   It's alright.

Ayeesha   Right, Evelyn is coming.

Evelyn *enters, slightly drunker than before.*

Evelyn   What do you want?

Ayeesha   Max, do you have your drink?

Max   Yeah.

David   What you doing, love?

Ayeesha   So everyone, everyone. Hi. I just thought to get
everyone together. You know, in the family. Well, this small
part of the family.

Evelyn   What about Martin?

Max   Don't wait for him.

Ayeesha   That hopefully one day I'd be lucky to join.

Evelyn   Why is she shouting?

Ayeesha   I just thought it'd be good to do a little McCarthy
family toast to John, the husband, the father, the
grandfather and the friend. To John.

All say 'To John' sporadically with some hesitance.

Evelyn   'Nothing is difficult for the strong and faithful.'

Ayeesha   What?

David   McCarthy family motto.

Evelyn   Bingo.

David   She has the coat of arms in the attic.

Ayeesha   It's a lovely motto, Evelyn. Poignant.

Evelyn   Not as good as my family name. Flanagan. 'I have fought and conquered.'

Ellis   Fitting.

Ayeesha   Shall we all get a photo together?

Evelyn   Ellis, I need to talk to you about something.

Ellis   Okay . . .

Evelyn   It's not a big deal but it's a little awkward so I wanted to . . . I know you'll want to know about the will.

Ellis   Erm, I wasn't really thinking /

Evelyn   It's just an important conversation to have so everyone's in the know.

Ayeesha   Should we leave her to it, love?

Evelyn   Her? Who's her?

David   You're being loud, Mam.

Evelyn   Let me speak.

Beat.

So basically, the will. You're not in it. Alright? And Max is. Cos Max is going to uni, your grandad really cared about that. I didn't want you to get your hopes up or anything or for you to get upset. Or hear from someone else your dad got this and Max got this etc. He loved you, Ellis. This changes nothing. So. We're all in the know now. Okay?

No response.

It's just money. You know?

Ellis Yeah, sure.

Evelyn Besides you get loads of money off your mam all the time.

Ellis What?

Evelyn Your dad says she sends you guilt money, doesn't she?

Ellis (*caught off guard*) Ohh. Okay.

David Haway, we'll go for a tab.

Evelyn I don't want to. I'm having a conversation, David. How is your mother, Ellis?

Ellis I wouldn't know.

Evelyn Where is she now? Is she still in Leeds?

Ellis Your guess is as good as mine, Evelyn.

Evelyn Is she still knocking about with that bloke?

Ellis I don't know.

Ayeesha Ellis and Max, shall we go get a drink? Apparently karaoke is starting.

Max Can I have another pint?

Evelyn When did you last speak to her?

Ellis She sent me a cryptic text message on my birthday three years ago.

Evelyn Not right for a mother to be like that.

Ellis Say again?

Evelyn Not right for a mother to be like that.

Ellis Listen, you're preaching to the converted.

Evelyn   Her family was a sight to behold. I don't know if you remember much about them.

Ellis   I do want a drink actually.

Ellis *goes to leave.*

Evelyn   I pray for you, you know, Ellis.

Ellis   Okay . . .

Evelyn   I do care for you. I helped raise you when she wouldn't.

Ellis   You've never mentioned.

Evelyn   Did you know that, Max? I was forced to look after your cousin when his mam didn't fancy it anymore.

Ellis   Forced? Okay, Evelyn.

Evelyn   Don't forget who your family is. You can have your big city life in London but you've got to remember those who matter.

Ellis   I haven't seen your sister, Grandma.

Evelyn   June's gone home, she was tired.

Ellis   No, no. Not Aunty June. Where's Aunty Jacqui?

Beat.

Shame she couldn't be here today, you know, to be with Grandad. He would've wanted that.

Evelyn *throws her glass of red and it splatters on the wall.*

She starts and doesn't stop.

Evelyn   OUT. OUT. GET OUT! HOW DARE YOU! GET OUT OF MY SIGHT.

David   Alright, outside! Come on, Mam.

David *holds* **Evelyn** *back and takes her through the outside door.*

A moment.

Ellis   At what point do we get the family photo?

Ayeesha *awkwardly smiles and exits.*

Ellis *goes back through to the party.*

Max *is left alone. They take a look at the scene of the wall and take a photo.*

Black out.

Act Two

The Wedding. Early 2020

'Saturday Night' by Whigfield plays at the party.

Ellis *enters on the phone.*

Ellis   Hiya. You must be at work. Don't worry about calling back. I've just been thinking about you a lot today. It's been weird, you know, being here for this. Feel a bit alone. But I'll see you when I get back. Hopefully. Have a good shift. You can ring back, if you want to. Okay. Bye.

He ends the message and begins to get upset. He goes to plate up some food and slowly starts to do the dance moves for 'Saturday Night' whilst still looking upset.

He takes his plate and sits in a chair in the corner of the room.

Ayeesha *enters in a wedding dress dragging* **David** *who's in a suit.*

Neither of them notice that **Ellis** *is in the room.*

Ayeesha (*shouting through the door*)   Thanks so much for coming, darling. Aw. Haha! Bless you. You are so so sweet. You owe me a dance!

She slams the door shut.

David   What's this about?

She snatches his drink off him and puts it down.

What's wrong?

Ayeesha   What the fuck was that?

David   Marty's speech?

Ayeesha   Yes, Martin's fucking speech.

David   I should have read it before.

Ayeesha   You didn't read it before?

David   It's supposed to be a surprise.

Ayeesha   He called me Diane twice and then basically called me a prostitute.

David   It wasn't that bad. Is a sugar baby the same thing as a prostitute?

Ayeesha   It was mortifying.

David   What do you want me to do?

Ayeesha   Keep him away from my sister for a start. If I don't tear him a new one, she will. Everything wrong. It's all wrong.

David   How?

Ayeesha   No one is dancing, your mother is walking around with a bloody urn and Max isn't even taking photos!

David   We've got a photographer for free! Stop complaining.

Ayeesha   I don't care.

David   Did you say my mam was carrying an urn?

Ayeesha   I can't believe you.

David   Look, I'll do my best to speak to her.

Ayeesha   David.

David   She doesn't talk to me.

Ayeesha   She's batshit crazy. Can you do it quickly? It's making me uncomfortable that the urn will be in all the photos. People think she's going to sprinkle your dad into the fucking food.

Ellis   By the taste of this sandwich I don't think she has.

Ayeesha   Ellis.

Ayeesha *smiles, stares at* **David** *then storms off.*

David   She's alright.

David *picks up his glass and leaves.*

Ellis *goes back to the table and begins to plate up.*

Evelyn *enters from outside carrying an urn.*

Evelyn   I always seem to find you at the buffet table.

Ellis   Nice hat, Grandma.

Evelyn   It is, isn't it?

Ellis   You kept my eyes out of the sun in the church like a parasol.

Evelyn   I'm pleased you did a reading. Even if it was from Moulin Rouge.

Ellis   It was the least I could do.

Evelyn   Yes, it was.

Ellis   I see you brought Grandad as your plus one.

Evelyn   I don't really understand your sense of humour, Ellis.

Ellis   Right.

Beat.

Evelyn   The decorations are a bit tacky.

Ellis   Didn't you pick them out?

Evelyn   Best I could find with the colour. What would possess someone to have purple as a colour scheme for their wedding? It's like a Dairy Milk advert in there.

Ellis   Dad seems happy.

Evelyn   Does he?

Ellis   I think so.

Evelyn   Let's hope it's his last attempt.

Ellis   Do you reckon there'll have kids?

Evelyn   Don't be daft. He's too old.

Ellis   But she isn't.

Evelyn   He's sat me away from the top table, you know? Well, I say 'he' did. Her Aunty and Martin up there.

Ellis   They put me on the kids' table so I wouldn't take offence.

Evelyn   The table is fine.

Ellis   Who you with?

Evelyn   Margaret, Simon, Frances and Duncan.

Ellis   Frances and Duncan?

Evelyn   Yep. They've been following me around all day. Don't how they dare show their faces.

Ellis   I thought you were in charge of the guestlist?

Evelyn   I didn't think they'd actually come. I invited them to be polite. Can you imagine what that witch would've said if I hadn't?

Ellis   Why?

Evelyn   Cos they're family. Technically. Your dad's always liked his uncle.

Ellis   You didn't need to invite them.

Evelyn   That's not how it works.

A moment.

He would've been mad about all this.

Ellis   Why?

Evelyn   Well, he'd already invested in two failed marriages. He used to say he would've preferred two holidays.

Ellis   Uncle Martin and Sarah were together for thirteen years.

Evelyn   Still a failed marriage.

Beat.

I've downsized, you know.

Ellis   I heard.

Evelyn   Did your dad pass on my new address?

Ellis   He did.

Evelyn   I thought he might have.

Ayeesha *enters.*

Ayeesha   Evelyn! There you are.

Evelyn   Were you looking for me?

Ayeesha   I feel like I haven't seen you all day.

Evelyn   Oh really.

Ayeesha   This week has been so nice, hasn't it? Been a while since we've all properly got together.

Evelyn   Yes.

Ayeesha   Can I just say, thank you again for the money you gave for the wedding.

Evelyn *raises her eyebrows.*

Ayeesha   Are you both having fun? Having a nice time?

Ellis   Yes.

Ayeesha   Great. I'm starving. I haven't had anything all day. I've barely had anything for the past three weeks. I've been juicing.

Ayeesha *starts eating. The chewing and swallowing keeps the conversation jolty.*

Ellis   The ceremony was beautiful.

Ayeesha   Thank you.

Evelyn   Nice of Max to take the photos.

Ayeesha   Max is a life saver. So many photos, I'm getting aches from all the smiling.

They all forcefully laugh.

Ayeesha   Has anyone seen Max? I need to talk to them.

Ellis   Probably somewhere taking photos.

Ayeesha   Probably.

Evelyn   It's a shame that June decided not to come. She's been watching the news too much, worried about getting sick.

Ayeesha   Bless her. It's a weird time, isn't it?

Evelyn   I see there's been some other no shows.

Ayeesha   I barely noticed. Such a crazy day.

Beat.

Not a lot of people are dancing. You should get everyone going, Ellis.

Ellis   Oh no, I'm all good.

Ayeesha   It'd be brilliant.

Ellis   That's okay.

Ayeesha   Why not? I don't understand, you're a dancer.

Evelyn   He works in recruitment.

Ayeesha   Recruit dancers then, ahhh!

Ellis   I actually don't work in recruitment anymore.

Evelyn   Why don't you get up in front of everyone like you used to do in my living room? You used to love being the centre of attention.

Ayeesha   Do I need to pay you or something? Is that why?

Ellis   I'd just rather not.

Ayeesha   Okay.

A moment.

So thoughtful of you to have John be a part of the day, Evelyn. That's so . . . special. It's really special.

Evelyn   What?

Ayeesha *gestures to the urn.*

Evelyn   Oh yes.

Ayeesha   It's a lovely urn.

Evelyn   Thank you.

Ayeesha   I hope it doesn't get damaged with you carrying it around.

Evelyn   It won't.

Ayeesha   Let's hope not.

David *enters.*

David   Mother.

Evelyn   David.

Ayeesha   I'll catch yous in a bit.

Ayeesha *exits after squeezing* **David***'s arm.*

Evelyn   Ellis, grab my bag will you? I'm going for a smoke.

Ellis *picks up the bag and hands it to her.*

David   Mam. Mam!

Evelyn   What?

David   Ellis, can we have a minute?

Ellis *exits.*

Evelyn   Make it brief, I'm dying for one.

David   This is silly. You're being silly, mother.

Evelyn   What are you on about?

David   Why did you bring that?

Evelyn   Him.

David   Fine. Why did you bring him?

Evelyn   Because I wanted to, David.

David   Why are you like this with me, Mam?

Evelyn   I don't know what you're talking about, David.

David   I think you do.

Beat.

Ever since Dad died, you want nothing to do with me. And I can take it any other day of the year but not today.

Evelyn   I helped pay for this wedding. I don't think it's a crime for me to want your dad to be here today.

David   It's making people uncomfortable.

Evelyn   Are you uncomfortable?

David   Yes, I am.

Beat.

Look, you wanted to make a point and it's been made /

Evelyn   I've not done anything.

David   Now can you just put it away for the rest of the evening?

Evelyn   Why?

David   Cos I've asked you nicely. It's my wedding day.

Pause.

Evelyn   I was chatting to Duncan.

David   Is this about your table?

Evelyn   And he said something odd to me.

David   What?

Evelyn   Thank you for doing what John would've wanted. He can be at peace now.

Beat.

David   What did he mean by that?

Evelyn   God's watching son.

A moment.

You are many things, David but I never thought you to be disloyal.

David   Christ almighty. You are on top form tonight.

Evelyn   Don't talk to your mother like that. If I spoke to my mother the way you often talk to me she would've beat me to a pulp.

Beat.

You admit it then.

Beat.

How could you do something like that to me? To him?

David   It was the right thing to do.

Evelyn   But I said, didn't I? I said I didn't want his ashes to be in Ireland with them lot. He would've said the same. You didn't know him like I did, David.

David   But it's a pile of dust, Mam. It's not him.

Evelyn   Is that what you're going to do to me when I'm nothing but dust? Give bits of me to whoever.

David   Duncan isn't no one.

Evelyn   He is to me.

David   Mam, come on. They're trying to make it right.

Evelyn   I shouldn't have invited them.

David   They're family.

Evelyn   Not my family.

David   You pick and choose when that word is important.

Evelyn   Oh, I have half a mind . . .

David   Go on.

Evelyn   I have half a mind to ask for my money back. Every sodding penny.

David   You can leave if you want. Go home. I wouldn't care.

Max *enters.*

Max   Ayeesha said I need a photo of the groom and his mother.

David   Max /

Evelyn   Go on, Max, I want to remember this moment.

They take the photo.

David *immediately exits back through to the party.*

Evelyn *makes her way out into the smoking area.*

Max *relaxes, finally away from the party.*

They spot the urn.

Max   Hello, Grandad.

Ellis *enters with two shots.*

Ellis   Here you go.

Max   What's this?

Ellis   A shot.

Max   But why?

Ellis   I missed your eighteenth.

Max   That was a year ago.

Ellis   Come on. Take the shot. I'm supposed to be your fun cousin who gets you drunk.

Max   You missed Christmas.

Ellis   Grandma was hosting so . . .

They do the shot.

Max   She left him.

Ellis   Who?

Max   She left the urn.

Ellis   Oh that. She's lost the plot. She's wearing a stupid hat as well.

Max   Don't be mean.

Ellis   She can't hear you.

Max   Okay yeah, maybe it is a bit weird but I don't know why you've got such a problem with her.

Ellis   She has a problem with me. She loves to talk about my eating.

Ellis *eats something from the table.*

The funny thing is I barely eat when I'm around her, the food is always shit. Except maybe the cold pizza and the quiche.

Max   I've never tried quiche.

Ellis   Quiche?

Max   Nope. Never tried it.

Ellis   You've grown up in this family and you have never had quiche. Why?

Max   It always makes me gip.

Ellis   I guess it does look quite sad.

Max   Bork.

Ellis   But it's not that bad.

Max   It is.

Ellis   You should try it. At least once.

Max   Nope.

Ellis   Come on.

Max   It looks like curdled milk.

Ellis   For me.

Max   Never.

Ellis   You would do it if Grandma asked you to.

Max   No I wouldn't.

Ellis   Alright, well do it for Grandad.

Ellis *picks up the urn and the ash pours out onto the floor.*

Okay.

Max   What the fuck?

Ellis   Okay.

Max   Ellis!

Ellis   Okay.

Max   Why would you do that?

Ellis   Oh you know, I just fancied seasoning the carpet. I think it's fucking obvious I didn't mean to do that, Max!

Max   Grandma is literally outside that door having a tab.

Ellis   Shit.

Max   Yeah.

Ellis   Well, come on then. Pick it up!

They both go to pick up the ashes with their hands but stop themselves.

Max   Jesus Christ.

Ellis   He's not going to help us right now!

Max   How do we pick it up?

Ellis   Paper plates. Get the paper plates.

Max *gets the plates.*

Max   Here.

Ellis   Quickly.

They begin to scoop up the ash and put it back into the urn.

Max   That sort of works. Wait.

Ellis   What?

Max   Just give me a second, there's something in my eye.

Ellis   Perfect.

Max   What?

Ellis   That'll be your grandad.

Max   This isn't happening.

Ellis   It definitely is.

Max   I think I'm going to cry.

Ellis   Can you do that somewhere else once we've finished? This is kind of important.

They finish scooping.

That's most of it.

Max   There's still some of it on the carpet.

Ellis   Just try to spread it out with your shoe.

Max   We're going to hell.

Ellis   Yeah, yeah, I look forward to it. Hurry up.

Max   Does it look okay?

Ellis   It's fine.

Max   It's still in my eye.

Ellis   Are you actually crying?

Max   Yes. Now put it back on the chair.

Ellis   Which chair?

Max   That chair.

Ellis   I need some specifics.

Max   I can't fucking see just pick one.

Ellis *puts the urn on a chair.*

Evelyn *enters.*

Ellis   Grandma.

Evelyn   What have you done?

Ellis   Nothing.

Evelyn   What's wrong with her?

Max   Them, Grandma.

Evelyn   Yes. Aw, I'm sorry, I'm sorry. What's wrong with them? Your eyes look a little bloodshot.

Max   I'm fine.

Ellis   They were crying.

Evelyn   What? Why?

Ellis   Seeing the urn. Just got a bit upset.

Evelyn   Oh love.

Evelyn *hugs* **Max**.

Max   I'll be okay.

Evelyn   Look, I'll put him away, shall I?

Max   Yeah.

Evelyn   Alright.

Evelyn *begins to leave.*

Evelyn   This carpet is filthy.

Evelyn *exits.*

Max   Ellis.

Ellis   What?

Max   You've got a bit of him . . . the ashes on your /

Max *wipes the ashes off* **Ellis***'s suit.*

Ellis   Great. I wanted to return this.

Max   The carpet.

Ellis   They'll hoover the rest of it up on Monday.

Max   Ellis!

Ellis   I know it's not ideal but I don't know what else to tell you.

Max   Grandad's going to end up in a Dyson?

Ellis   Jesus. I need to get drunk.

Max   So do I.

Beat.

Give us those shot glasses.

He does.

Max *pulls a bottle of sambuca out of their bag from under the table.*

Ellis   Erm. What the fuck?

Max   I've been mixing it with my lime and soda.

Ellis   Max! You're supposed to be at work!

Max   Piss off. It's a wedding.

Ellis   What is it?

Max   Sambuca.

Ellis   I'd rather shit in my hands and clap.

Max *begins to pour the shots.*

Max   Come on. I stole it from Grandma's cabinet.

Ellis   Excuse me?

Max   She doesn't drink it. It's for decoration.

Ellis   You little rebel. Uni has changed you.

Max   Shut up.

Ellis   And here I thought I was the bad influence.

Max *offers* **Ellis** *the shot.*

Ellis   Fine.

They do the shot.

Throughout the scene, **Max** *and* **Ellis** *take shots.*

Sometimes together, sometimes alone.

Ellis   I'd have never done that at your age.

Max   Why?

Ellis   I don't know. I've just always felt the need to impress Grandma, even though she's a bit of cunt.

Max   Woah!

Ellis   Oh calm down, I only said 'a bit'.

A moment.

Max   Ellis. What happened? With Grandad and Aunty Jacqui?

Ellis   Your dad won't tell you.

Max   I'm scared to ask him.

Ellis   What do you think?

Max   I don't know.

Ellis   Do you want to know?

No response.

To tell you the truth, I don't know. Well, I don't know all of it. I know they had an affair. I don't know for how long. I don't know when Grandma found out. But I do know when other people started to find out, she did something about it. At one point Aunty Jacqui was at every family event and one day she wasn't.

Pause.

The older you get, you start to learn about all the family drama. I used to be the young 'un who wasn't told any of it. And now I am the drama.

Max   What have you done like?

Ellis   The first gay in the family.

Max   Oh.

Ellis   And it still makes people uncomfortable.

Max   I think your dad is over it.

Ellis   You would say that. He's not. He might think he is but he's not.

Max   Why?

Ellis   For one, he doesn't talk about it.

Max   He's quiet.

Ellis   That's intentional. He doesn't have me on social media, you know.

Max   What?

Ellis   It's funny.

Max   Does he even use it?

Ellis   Enough. He just doesn't want to see my life.

Max   I'm sure that's not /

Ellis   You put him on a pedestal.

Max   No, I don't.

Ellis   Yes, you do.

Max   You're too hard on him.

Ellis   Try having him as a dad.

Max   I would. You don't know how lucky you are.

Ellis   Ah, I see. You think my issues with my dad don't really matter cos he doesn't have a drinking problem?

Max   Alright, Ellis.

Ellis   What?

Max   I can say things like that. You can't.

Beat.

Ellis   Does he try to change you? Your dad.

Max   I keep myself to myself.

Ellis   So he ignores you.

Max   I ignore him. Your dad doesn't ask you to change.

Ellis   Not in those words. I tone it down for his and everyone else's comfortability. And I'm a bit sick of doing that.

Ellis *goes to continue but stops himself.*

Max   What?

Ellis   I don't think I want to be here. I think I'm done.

Max   It's barely late.

Ellis   I don't mean tonight.

Max   What do you mean then?

Ellis   I mean here. Home. The family.

Max   Okay?

Ellis   You know it's crossed my mind a few times.

Max   What has?

Ellis   To not be a part of it.

Max   Oh. You mean like leave the family?

Ellis   Well, it wouldn't be so official.

Max   You're being serious?

Ellis   You don't choose your family but you can choose to be around them.

Max   You can't do that.

Ellis   I don't owe them anything, I'm not responsible for anything. If you never saw me again, it wouldn't make a difference.

Max   I don't think that.

Ellis   I have my life. I don't depend on anyone else. I have friends. Some who don't speak to their families.

Max   But /

Ellis   But what? Blood's thicker than water?

Beat.

Max   You can't just leave your family.

Ellis   But that's the thing, I think you fully can. I know you wouldn't but you're a peacekeeper.

Max   A what?

Ellis   A peacekeeper. You rarely pick a side. You don't want to be involved.

Max   You say that like it's a bad thing.

Ellis   It's not. You're better than me. Probably.

Max   So what would you do?

Ellis   I'd do what they do. I just wouldn't talk about it. I'd not come home and I wouldn't say a word. And neither would anyone else.

Beat.

One day you might feel the same.

Max   Bit condescending.

Ellis   But it's also true.

Max   I think it's sad.

Ellis   It is. And I've not felt a part of this family for a long time.

Max   How?

Ellis   You weren't around when Lisa was on the scene.

Max   Your mam?

Ellis   You won't remember her. I barely do. I haven't seen her since I was about fifteen. Well, I saw her once in town a few years ago but she didn't see me. Grandma was obviously buzzing when she was no longer around the family. My mam always gave everyone something to talk about. She would drop me off at family parties in dirty clothes after having me. My primary school once called my dad in cos Lisa had dropped me off at school with vodka in my water bottle. And then there's obviously Grandma's theory.

Max   What theory?

Ellis   When I was younger Grandma Evelyn didn't buy me Christmas presents. Grandad would slip me sweets and that but I got nothing proper from the two of them. My dad would kick off about it. He thought it was punishment for having a kid outside of wedlock but that wasn't the reason. Bless little me, I cried one year to my dad thinking I'd done something wrong to upset them. Cos you know, all the other kids at school would get things off their grandparents. Then I heard an argument where she said it out loud. It was here actually. Grandad's sixtieth. It all kicked off when my dad asked why Grandma told me to start calling her 'Evelyn'.

Max   Why?

Ellis   Cos she thinks that my dad isn't actually my dad.

Ellis *finds this funny,* **Max** *doesn't.*

Max   What?

Ellis   I probably shouldn't be telling you this.

Max   Are you serious?

Ellis   Yeah. It's why everyone's always acted weird around me, Max. She planted the seed. She doesn't think I'm family. Being gay just gave her even more of an excuse not to like me.

Max   So is he your dad?

Ellis   Who knows?

Max   Well, what do you think?

Ellis   If he's not then maybe I shouldn't be here.

Max   He is. He has to be.

Ellis   Yeah, probably.

Max   Shit.

Ellis   Yep.

Max   I didn't realise.

Ellis   Realise what?

Max   All of it.

Ellis   Like I say, the older you get. Forgive me if I think blood's not thick enough.

David *enters, drunk.*

Max *hides the sambuca.*

David   What are you two doing in here instead of out there?

Max   There's food.

David   The food? It's crap. Ayeesha's family aren't eating any of it, your grandma is furious.

David *laughs. He gets really close to* **Ellis**.

Beat.

Ellis   You having fun?

David   Of course. More fun than you are.

Ellis   What?

David   You're in a mood.

Ellis   No, I'm not.

David   Hanging out in here most of today. Cos you're in a mood with me.

Ellis   Am I?

David   I haven't asked. I haven't done the thing. Is that it?

Ellis   What?

David   Do you need any money? Have you done anything illegal? I forgot, shoot me.

Ellis   Why don't you go back to the party?

David   What's wrong? Are you not happy for me?

Ellis   I'm really happy for you. Ayeesha looks lovely.

David   She does, you're right.

Ellis   Where is she?

David   What did I do now? To upset you.

Ellis   What do you mean?

David   I'm always upsetting him, Max. I've always done something wrong. And he waits for me to figure it out. His mam used to do that when we were seeing each other.

Ellis   Right.

David   I remember one time she was in a mood with me for a couple of days. We met at the pub and she had no craic, was being all blunt and barely touched her pint. And you know what it was? She was pregnant. And she was mad at me about it. Blaming me. It was weird. Acting like she wasn't the one who wanted to have sex in the first place.

Ellis   Okay, Dad.

David   Your grandma was so angry with me when she found out. She didn't talk to me for months. My dad begged me to marry her. But I couldn't do it cos I could tell from a mile off she was going to fuck up my life. We were kids really. Of course Grandma couldn't stand her and vice versa. At the time, Grandma didn't tell anyone, you know, about the pregnancy. And then when you came along she was telling everyone I was getting married and I wasn't. Complete denial. And it's funny that you went into dancing and all that cos I wanted to call you Billy. And obviously we didn't in the end but anyway I told people that I wanted to and then your mam was mad at me again. But I didn't know why. I had to figure it out. Do all the guess work. Then I'd say sorry. Most of the time I wouldn't mean it but I couldn't be arsed with the drama. So what do I have to say sorry for now? Come on. I'll do my best to mean it.

Ellis   You had a bit to drink?

David   It's my wedding day. What did you expect?

Max   Should I go?

David   No, Max-a-million, it's fine. It's fine. Besides I want a witness.

Ellis   Dad, you're making a fool out of yourself.

Ayeesha *enters.*

Ayeesha   We're cutting the cake soon, they're bringing it to our table. Max, you need to be taking more photos.

David   Give us a second.

Ayeesha   What's going on?

David   Ellis was about to tell me why he's in a mood.

Ellis   I'm not in a mood.

David   He is.

Ayeesha   He said he isn't in a mood, darling. Come on.

David   What's the issue then?

Ellis   I'm not going to spoil your day.

David   Just tell me. You're pissing me off now.

Ayeesha   David.

Ellis   Okay, fine.

David   What?

Ellis   The invitation.

David   What about it?

Ellis   Do I need to spell it out?

David   If you don't mind.

Ellis   Plus one. 'Ellis plus one.'

David   Right?

Ayeesha   We thought it'd be nice to invite him.

Ellis   Aw, it's nice, yeah. Was it that hard to write his name?

Ayeesha   I just thought he might not have been able to make it so you might have wanted to invite a friend.

Ellis   Bullshit.

David   Don't talk to my wife like that.

Ellis   We've been together for years and you don't meet him, don't ask about him and now you don't even acknowledge he has a name.

David   You're being dramatic, Ellis.

Ellis   His name is Alex. Does that make you uncomfortable?

David   Don't be so stupid.

Ellis   It's a genuine question. I don't understand why you wouldn't just put it on the invitation.

David   It doesn't. Like you say, I've just never met him.

Ellis   Say his name then, Dad. Say it.

David   This is pathetic. You're being childish.

Ellis   You think you're so mature?

Max   Ellis.

Ellis   No one's going to die, Dad. Saying his name isn't going to make you gay.

David   Why didn't you bring him?

Ellis   He wasn't exactly going to get the warmest welcome, was he?

David   I think you're embarrassed of this family.

Ellis   You might be onto something there.

David   Think you're better than everyone, don't you?

Ayeesha   Stop it now. The pair of you.

Ellis   I couldn't bring Alex anyway.

David   Why's that?

Ellis   Cos we broke up a year ago. But you know, you wouldn't know that cos you never asked about him. You never tried to meet him, you didn't care.

Beat.

I know, I know. You would've preferred it if he wasn't a man /

David   Oh here we go.

Ellis   Am I wrong?

David   You know, being gay isn't a personality, Ellis.

Ellis   What?

David   Sometimes you need to learn to shut up, son. You walk around playing the victim all the time. It's embarrassing.

A moment.

Ellis   Fuck you.

David   You what?

Ellis   Fuck you.

David *grabs* **Ellis** *by the scruff of his neck.*

David   You talk to your dad like that, ey? You talk to your dad like that!

Ayeesha   David!

Ellis   What are you going to do?

Evelyn *enters.*

Ayeesha   Stop it. Get off him. Everyone can hear you.

Evelyn   David.

David *lets go of* **Ellis**. *Everyone stops.*

Evelyn   Clean yourself up, you're a mess. Your poor wife.

A moment.

David *exits.*

Ellis   You can tell him he'll never fucking see me again. Do you hear that?

Ayeesha *glares at* **Ellis.**

She takes a moment to ready herself then goes back into the party.

Max   Are you okay? Ellis?

Evelyn   Come on. You need to get in there and take a photo of the happy couple cutting the cake.

Ellis (*aside*)   Being a peacekeeper is a bad thing, Max. Grow up and eat the fucking quiche.

Max   I think I need to be sick.

Max *exits.*

Evelyn *gets out cigarettes.*

Evelyn   You want a tab?

No response. She lights up.

Okay.

Ellis   You're smoking in here?

Evelyn   It's freezing out there. Who in their right mind gets married in February?

A moment.

It's not a real wedding if there's no kick off. I remember your dad and Diane's wedding.

Ellis   I should probably /

Evelyn   I'm about to tell an interesting story, Ellis.

Ellis   Oh sorry.

Evelyn   You were barely ten. Louise and Helen were bridesmaids cos Diane's nieces weren't that pretty. Her dress was awful.

Ellis   Hideous. I remember it.

Evelyn   No wonder they didn't last. I remember at the reception when you smashed one of her wedding presents on the dance floor to try to make Louise and Helen laugh. You were quite naughty as a kid. I blame your mother for that. It was this porcelain angel with some saying on it. A tacky dust collector Diane would've stuck on the mantelpiece, nowt special. I grabbed you by the wrist, dragged you to their table and made you say sorry to her. It ruined her day. And she hated you after that.

Ellis   I quite liked Diane.

Evelyn   I don't know why. She was dull. There's nothing more offensive you can be.

Beat.

Your grandad said I should have never told her.

Ellis   Why?

Evelyn   You were just a child then. You didn't know any better. Well, that's what he said.

Evelyn *puts out the cigarette on the buffet table.*

She goes to exit but stops herself.

How's my sister?

Ellis   What?

Evelyn   You think I'm stupid, Ellis?

Ellis   I would never say you are.

Evelyn   You've been to visit her.

No response.

Don't bother lying to me.

Ellis   We've spoken a few times.

Evelyn   I wondered how she got my new address.

Ellis   She wanted to reach out.

Evelyn   I didn't read it. How is she?

Ellis   She's been ill but she's getting better . . . I think you should /

Evelyn   Don't tell me what you think I should do.

Beat.

Tell her I said you're a stranger to me now.

Ellis   I think she knows that.

Evelyn   I'm not talking about her.

Beat.

I gave so much to you, Ellis. So much you don't even realise. But now you're a stranger. So I'll be polite but from now on, that's all you'll get from me.

Evelyn *exits.*

Outside we hear the party cheer.

Ellis *toasts and downs the rest of his drink and exits.*

Ayeesha *is on the platform with the microphone.*

Ayeesha   Oh my god. Hi. Hello everyone. Wow. I know we've already had some speeches and weren't they just great. Martin, our Marty. What a guy. Oo, I'll get you for that one. I know it's not traditional for the bride to do a speech but this is my moment! Let me have it! Haha! Those who know me know I usually hate public speaking, so I won't keep you for long, especially since there's now cake! Made by gorgeous sister, Khadeeja. I love you! I just wanted to say, thank you all so much for being a part of my sorry . . .

our haha . . . special day. I'm the happiest woman on earth, I could just scream. It's been . . . perfect. I know the world is a weird place at the minute. I don't care what anyone says, no matter how bad this thing gets, I've worked very hard on this wedding and I will not cancel my honeymoon next month! Haha! They can't stop me! But while that's all kicking off around the globe, it's good to be with family. And not all of mine could make it but you know, that's fine. And there's some other loved ones who we wish were still with us like John. But despite that, I feel so surrounded by love. I mean who else can say they've been walked down the aisle by someone as beautiful as my Aunty. And now I'm in this whacky family. Haha! I'm a McCarthy! Well, it's double barrelled but still. It's a new adventure. I'm an honorary northerner. And I said it would happen, didn't I? David was tough one to convince but, in the end, he had to. And that makes me so so happy. And we are here today in the place where the family has always been and always will be. A toast to this place. Cheers! Please eat. Drink! And I just want to finish off by saying David, I love you, darling and I owe you a dance.

'Five Hundred Miles' by the Proclaimers plays.

Come here! Come on. It's the song, David! Surprise! Someone push him. Why are you being shy? Come on. He's so silly.

David *joins her.*

Ayeesha   Here he is! Please don't let us be alone on the dance floor!

She dances with **David** *and no one joins.*

Ayeesha   Come on. Let's dance. Why is no one dancing? What? Get up. What's wrong? Why is no one dancing? Why is no one dancing? It's weird. This is a wedding. It's my wedding day.

David *begins to usher her off.*

Ayeesha   Why is no one dancing?! Just fucking get up. Dance! DANCE!

They exit.

Blackout.

Act Three

The Christening. Early 2022

A baby is crying. **David** *is alone with a baby carrier.*

He does his best to get the baby to settle.

David   Ey, ey. Come on little one. Come on. What you crying for? What's going on? Ey? What's all the fuss about? Yes I know, I know. It's all a bit much, isn't it? Is it too loud? The DJ has got a bad taste in music, doesn't he? Doesn't he? Come on. Shhh. Are you tired? Do you want to go to sleep? Ey, shhh. That's it. Shhh.

The baby gets louder.

David   Ah fucking hell. Right. It's okay, you don't need to cry. Look who's here? It's me! You know me. Who is it? Ey? Is it your dad? Is it your dad? That's right. It's your dad, Mia.

The baby begins to settle.

David   Shhh. Oh, are you a little sleepy sausage? Yes, you are. You are, Mia. Shhh.

The baby is quiet.

Max *enters abruptly.*

Max   Fancy a pint, Uncle David?

David *shoots them a look, miming the baby is asleep.*

Max (*whispered*)   Oh. Sorry. Do you fancy a pint, Uncle David?

The two whisper for the rest of the conversation.

David   Yes.

Max   What do you want?

David   Guinness, please.

Max   What?

David   Guinness.

Max   They're out.

David   Carling then.

Max   Carling?

David   Yes.

Max *goes to leave.*

David   Max.

Max   What?

David   Tell Ayeesha that Mia is asleep.

Max   Mia needs what?

David   Asleep.

Max   She needs to sleep?

David   No. She is asleep.

Max   She is asleep.

David   Yes, tell her.

Max   Mia is asleep.

Ayeesha *enters.*

Ayeesha   Is she asleep?

Max *and* **David** *signal for her to be quiet.* **Ayeesha** *freezes.* **David** *checks on* **Mia**.

They start to come out of the whisper.

David   She's down.

They relax. **Max** *exits.*

Ayeesha   Thank you.

Ayeesha *hugs* **David**.

David   Ey, I'm getting good.

Ayeesha   You are.

David   Like riding a bike.

Ayeesha   It suits you. Being a dad.

David   I've always been a dad.

Ayeesha   I know but it's different.

David   I could do this all on my own.

Ayeesha   Could you now?

David   You bet.

Ayeesha   Perfect, I fancied a break from breastfeeding.

They laugh.

Ayeesha   Quite the party in there.

David   No wonder she was crying.

Ayeesha   Booziest christening I've ever been to.

David   You know my family, any excuse.

Beat.

David   Does today feel sad to you?

Ayeesha   What do you mean?

David   I don't know. I guess it's just the first time
everyone's got together in a while. You can feel who's
missing, you know. No Aunty June, Uncle Michael's in a
home, Ellis didn't come.

Ayeesha   We knew that might happen.

David   Yeah, yeah.

Ayeesha   And your mam?

David   Yeah. Martin keeps talking about her. I think it's
upsetting Max.

Ayeesha   You okay darling?

David   I'm alright.

Ayeesha   You sure?

David   I am . . . it's sad obviously . . . her not being here . . . feels strange . . . it's . . .

Ayeesha   I know.

David   It's just hit me.

Ayeesha   What?

David   I really need the loo.

Ayeesha   Wait. Whilst she's asleep, should we get the photo?

David   Let's do it in a bit, I need the loo.

Ayeesha   But when?

David   After I've had a piss would be preferable.

Ayeesha   But now is the best time, she's settled. She's crying in all the other ones.

Max *enters with a drink.*

Ayeesha   Look, Max is here.

Max   Here you go.

Max *goes to give* **David** *the pint.*

David   Cheers Max, just put it down there.

Max   Ayeesha, some of your work friends are heading off.

David   Go say bye to them. I'm going to the loo.

Ayeesha   They can wait. Could you just hold it in?

David   I have for the last half an hour when I've been getting her to sleep.

Ellis *enters holding a present.*

Ellis   Sorry, I'm late.

Ayeesha   Ellis.

Ellis   I know I missed the ceremony. Big delay on the train. I should've messaged.

Pause.

Ellis   I brought this for . . .

Beat.

Ayeesha   Thank you.

Ayeesha *takes the present off* **Ellis**.

David   I'm going to piss myself.

David *exits.*

Ellis   I like your dress, Ayeesha.

Ayeesha   Thank you.

Ellis   How's it all been?

Ayeesha   It's been alright.

Ellis   I'm sorry I didn't come home sooner to see her.

Ayeesha   Yeah, I'd offer for you to hold her but she's sleeping so . . .

Ellis   Yeah, yeah.

Ayeesha   I need to say bye to a few friends. Max, could you . . .

Max   I'll stay with her.

Ayeesha   Would you mind actually? Just whilst she's sleeping. Only for five, ten minutes max, Max.

Max   Yeah sure.

Ayeesha   Thank you.

Ayeesha *exits.*

Max *and* **Ellis** *stare at the carrier for a moment.*

Ellis   Still the unofficial family photographer, I see.

Max   If I get paid.

Ellis   Oh. Do you actually do this now?

Max   Sort of. I work as an assistant for a media company. It's all corporate stuff, nothing exciting.

Ellis   Oh wow.

Max   What about you? Still dancing?

Ellis   No I don't do that anymore. Well I teach at a dance school part time but yeah . . . wasn't meant to be.

Max   How's it feel?

Ellis   What?

Max   To be a big brother?

Ellis   Fine, I guess. She's cute.

Max   She is for a baby.

Ellis   All babies are cute.

Max   Babies are ugly, we're all lying to ourselves.

Ellis   What's wrong with you?

Max   Me? I'm fine.

Beat.

Max   I didn't think you'd be here. It's been a while. I thought when things went back to normal, you'd come home.

Beat.

Max   Grandma's not here.

Ellis   Yeah. I didn't see her.

Max   She didn't want to come.

Ellis   Why?

Max   Did your dad not tell you? They don't talk anymore, Ellis.

Ellis   What?

Max   She's not well.

Ellis   What do you mean?

Max   It's ever since grandad died. Then Aunty June. She was devastated that she couldn't go to the funeral. I think she's lost it a bit.

Ellis   Do you think?

Max   She's not herself. So paranoid. Picks fights with everyone over nothing. I tried to talk to Uncle David about it but he doesn't care, my dad doesn't know what I'm on about and everyone else swears she's fine.

Ellis   She probably is.

Max   You haven't seen what she's been like. I don't know. I mean would you be surprised? All that time she had alone.

Beat.

Max   We had a drink one night and she told me she's been sending letters to Aunty Jacqui.

Ellis   Really? She said that?

Max   Said it was like it was nothing.

Ellis   For how long?

Max   She sent her some a couple of months ago. Why?

Ellis   Nothing . . . Just surprised.

Max   I think she's lonely.

Beat.

Ellis   Is it bad that I'm relieved?

Max   About what?

Ellis   That she's not here I mean.

Max   Just 'cos you don't like her. You don't like anyone.

Ellis   What?

Max   Am I wrong? You don't even like me.

Ellis   What?

Max   I don't think you do.

Ellis   That's not true.

Max   Yeah, it is.

Ellis   How?

Max   I message you, Ellis. You don't respond. You only speak to me at these things 'cos you have no one else to talk to.

Ellis   Right.

Max   It's not like we talk when you're not at home.

Beat.

Ellis   What would it mean if I didn't? Serious question. We're family, we don't have to like each other.

Max   Why?

Ellis   Why what?

Max   Why don't you like me?

Ellis   It's not that big of a deal, if I didn't.

Max   But why?

Ellis   Look, you are ten years younger than me and used to be my weird little cousin who didn't talk.

Max   Go straight for the jugular, jesus.

Ellis   I mean sure. Yeah. I like you.

Max   God. Okay.

Max *goes to leave.*

Ellis   Max, come on.

Max   Is that the only reason?

A moment.

Max   Use your words.

Ellis   Okay . . . Nobody cares about you.

Max   Erm thanks?

Ellis   You know about you being *you*. You've always been accepted. Nobody cared. It's chill. Everyone is so well-adjusted. No big drama. So yeah maybe, I kind of resent you for that.

Max   That's what you think?

Ellis   But the more I've thought about it, the more it makes sense. You came out much later than me so . . .

Max   So?

Ellis   Well things are different now. 2008 was a very different time.

Max   And I have it easy now?

Ellis   Maybe.

Max   You don't know anything, Ellis. You're never here.

Ellis   I know enough. I know you have it different from me.

Max   You're right, it is different. Me coming out may not have been what you went through but it wasn't easy. It's not an accident at every family party I spend most of the night in here. You know, when everyone is drinking they very quickly forget my name is Max. Especially my dad.

Ellis   But it's not this drama.

Max   I keep myself to myself. Maybe you should do the same.

Ellis   You get away with things I wouldn't be able to.

Max   Get away with things?

Ellis   'Cos you're the favourite.

Max   I'm not the favourite either.

Ellis   That's what the favourite would say.

Max   How am I the favourite?

Ellis   This really isn't up for debate.

Max   No, no. Tell me.

Ellis   Okay. The will?

Max   I knew you were going to say that.

Ellis   And?

Max   That was for uni, Ellis.

Ellis   It was more than that and you know it.

Max   No it wasn't.

Ellis   Didn't you drop out?

Max   Yeah.

Ellis   Why?

Max   Personal reasons. You would know why if you actually spoke to me.

Ellis   What? So I could be there for you? Is that what you mean? Like you've never been there for me, Max.

Max   Is that it? You don't like me 'cos I'm 'a peacekeeper' or whatever you called me?

Ellis   Maybe.

Max   For fucks sake, get over it. Why is it bad to want people to get along?

Ellis No, no it's good. It's good to just stand there and do nothing.

Beat.

Ellis I mean it would be nice if someone stood up for me for once. If someone was in my corner. But even the person who probably understands me the most, does nothing.

Max You think we're the same, Ellis? We're not. Not in the slightest. Yeah we used to joke about you being a good gay role model but you'll never get what I've gone through. It's completely different. So stop treating it like it's the same.

No response.

Max Can I be honest? I don't think the problem is that I'm the youngest or the favourite. I think you still feel guilty for being gay. And I think you're mad 'cos I don't feel guilty.

The baby cries.

A moment.

Ayeesha *enters.*

Ayeesha Is she alright? I heard her crying.

Max She just woke up.

Ayeesha *takes her out of the baby carrier.*

Ayeesha Mamma Mia! What are you crying for now darling? You need sleep, my gorgeous girl. Shhh. I'm here. It's okay. I'm here. Bless you. Aww. Do you need your dad? Where's your dad? Where's your dad gone?

The baby settles.

David *enters.*

David She woke up?

Ayeesha Yeah but she's fine. I've got her.

Max Do yous want the family photo now?

Ayeesha   Yes, Max. That would be great. David, let me be on the left.

David   Does it matter?

Ayeesha   Of course it does.

David   Right.

Ayeesha   Have I got food in my teeth?

David   What?

Ayeesha   Have I got food in my teeth?

David   No. Come on.

Ayeesha   Max, is the lighting alright?

Max   It's . . .

Ayeesha   Forget it. Let's just go.

Ellis   Did you want me to . . .

Ayeesha   Just the three of us for now.

Beat.

Ayeesha   We can get one later.

Ellis   Oh no, it's fine.

Ellis *takes a step back.*

Max   Mia, look at me!

Ayeesha   Smile Mia. Are you going to smile at Max? David help.

David   Look at Max, Mia.

Ayeesha   Gorgeous girl, smile!

Max *takes the photo.*

Evelyn *enters carrying a cake box.*

Evelyn   Hello.

Max   Grandma?

David   Mam.

Evelyn   I brought a cake.

Ayeesha   You're here?

Evelyn   People normally say thank you. Aw, my Max. You look wonderful. Give us a kiss.

Evelyn *kisses* **Max** *on the cheek.*

Ayeesha   We thought you weren't coming.

Evelyn   And not be here for my granddaughter?

Evelyn *goes over to* **Ayeesha.**

Evelyn   Oh, would you look at that. Such a chunky little thing. You should take off that stupid bow on her head, Ayeesha. The poor thing looks gift wrapped.

Ayeesha   David.

David   Why are you here, Mam?

Evelyn   Thought I'd stop by.

David   What's going on?

Evelyn   What's wrong with everyone? I brought a bloody cake.

David   You told us you didn't want to come. You told many people you didn't want to.

Evelyn   Well I'm here now and I'm not here for you. I've come to see my granddaughter.

Ayeesha   She needs to sleep.

Evelyn   Oh. Are you trying to keep her from me? Didn't think of bringing her to visit me and now I'm not allowed to hold her.

David   I'd like you to leave.

Evelyn   What?

David   I said I'd like you to leave.

Evelyn   Right. Stop this, David. I've brought a cake. Max, pass me the plates.

David   It's too late. I don't care if you want to be here now. I know you, mam. You've been saying all sorts about us to everyone. Then you didn't come to the christening to hurt me. To show me up. To make it all about you even when you weren't here.

Evelyn   I don't know how you dare after everything you've done to me.

David   What have I done?

Evelyn   You're trying to get rid of me. You left me to be alone for months on end. Then you go and move further out to get away from me once I stopped driving. Bet it was your idea, ey?

Ayeesha   It was actually.

Evelyn   She's manipulative. I said it from the start she's trying to take you away from me, David.

Ayeesha   She's deluded.

Evelyn   What was that?

Ayeesha   I said you're deluded. You're the one who refused to talk to us, Evelyn.

Evelyn   I had my reasons.

Ayeesha   What reasons?

Evelyn   I was waiting for an apology.

David   No, what you wanted was for me to come begging on my hands and knees for your forgiveness. But I won't. Not for you.

Evelyn   Don't you mean she won't let you?

Ayeesha Yeah sure, whatever.

Evelyn You've really got your nails in him, Ayeesha.

Max Grandma!

Ayeesha You're the one with the problem Evelyn. No one else.

David If it was up to you, I'd say sorry to you everyday and never stop.

Evelyn No you wouldn't, you're too proud. Too stubborn.

David I wonder who I get that from.

Evelyn You can go on about me trying to hurt you, David. But what about all the things you've done to hurt me over the years? Your own mother. I know what your father would say. You're nothing but a disappointment.

Max SHUT UP! Shut up. You're making everything worse. Just shut up!

Beat.

Max Go home, Grandma.

Evelyn *slams the cake box onto the table, trashing the buffet.*

Evelyn I know what you did as well.

Max Grandma, please.

Ellis Me?

Evelyn Yes, you Ellis.

Ellis I've not done anything.

Evelyn I tried to make it right. But you couldn't let me, could you?

Ellis I don't know what you mean.

Evelyn You told her not to reply to my letters. Didn't you? Didn't you?

David   What is she on about?

Ellis   Aunty Jacqui.

Evelyn   He goes to visit her.

Ellis   I don't.

Evelyn   Liar.

Ellis   I don't visit anymore.

Evelyn   Is that right?

Ellis   Yes.

Evelyn   He's lying.

Ellis   She died, Grandma.

Evelyn   What?

Ellis   A few months ago.

A moment.

Evelyn   I'm not having this/

Max   Grandma.

Evelyn   *gets the paper plates and starts to cut up the cake.*

Evelyn   I bought this cake. Come on. Who wants a slice? Come on, I spent money on this. It needs eating. Max? David? Who wants some cake?

Beat.

Evelyn   WHO WANTS SOME BLOODY CAKE?!

The baby starts to cry.

Ayeesha *exits with Mia.* **Ellis** *follows. Then* **Max**.

Evelyn *begins to eat a slice and* **David** *watches from afar.*

He goes to move towards her but she stands and stares at him.

Evelyn *exits.*

David *alone, he takes a drink of his abandoned pint.*

Ayeesha *enters holding* **Mia**.

Ayeesha   I just saw her leave. David, are you okay?

He kisses **Mia** *on her head.*

Ellis *enters.*

Ellis   Dad, I need to /

David   Not now, son.

David *exits.*

Ayeesha *puts* **Mia** *back in the baby carrier.*

A long awkward pause.

Ellis   How was the christening?

Ayeesha *goes to laugh.*

Ayeesha   Long and boring.

Ellis   Oh.

Ayeesha   Not worth it really. I mean I guess it'll help her get into a good school at one point or something stupid. The whole thing is hilarious.

Ellis   What do you mean?

Ayeesha   I didn't want to do it.

Ellis   Why did you then?

Ayeesha   Your dad wanted to. For her.

Ellis   What?

Ayeesha   This christening. He wanted to please Evelyn even though she wasn't there. Can you believe that?

Ellis   Yes.

Ayeesha   That woman has got this hold on him that he can't seem to shake. I used to be like that.

Ellis   Like what?

Ayeesha   I was desperate for Evelyn to like me but that was never going to happen, was it?

Beat.

Ayeesha   Look at this. What a fucking mess. I knew something like this would happen, why did we bother? Other than an excuse for people to drink?

Ellis   It's the culture.

Ayeesha   I'm not religious, neither is your dad.

Ellis   He might not be religious but it's still in him though. The guilt.

Ayeesha   It's in you aswell. All of you. You're all so het up about everything. People barely like eachother but everyone insists on spending time together. So much pressure for everyone to enjoy themselves. I've found myself getting caught up in it. 'It's just what you do', 'It's the done thing'.

Beat.

Ayeesha   He thinks you want to disown your family. Your dad.

Ellis   Right.

Ayeesha   Well you did say you were never going to see him again . . . at my wedding.

No response.

Ayeesha   Do you? You know what, I don't care. Do what you want.

Ellis   Erm.

Ayeesha   We don't need to talk about it. It's not like you like me.

Ellis   That's not /

Ayeesha You tolerate me. I get it. I do. You've had different versions of a mam in your life coming and going. Lisa, Diane. Even Evelyn.

Ellis I'm sure my dad has told you about my mam.

Ayeesha Dribs and drabs.

Ellis When they split up, I'd go back and forth between hers and my dad's. She was seeing this guy who was not a very nice man. I didn't like him and he didn't like having this little camp kid prancing around his house. And when it came down to Lisa staying with him or kicking me out, I found myself out on the street. All my stuff in a duvet cover waiting for my dad to pick me up. Nine years old. Grandma looked after me most of the time for a few years but didn't like me. Lisa tried to have some sort of relationship with me when I was a teenager but I stopped that. 'Cos she is the way she is. And my mam wasn't on drugs. She might have drank but not as much as Uncle Martin does. She just didn't want me. I'm sick of being rejected, Ayeesha. Sick of not being wanted. Every time I come home, I leave feeling worse about myself. I don't feel welcome here.

Ayeesha And you all made me feel welcome?

A moment.

Ayeesha I don't blame you for not wanting to be a part of it. This family is cold. Very white. And you all smell the same. It's weird. I smell amazing.

Ellis You do. I have always thought that.

Ayeesha It's an M&S own brand but stays on very well.

Ellis Nice.

Ayeesha And what is it with these parties? The same place with the same, shitty buffet. I don't get it really. It's food you've made hot to then make cold again. Stupid.

Ellis I guess it's the done thing.

Beat.

Ellis   He hasn't rang me since the wedding. You know, to talk. He used to ring quite a lot.

Ayeesha   It upset him when you never answered his calls.

Ellis   Did he tell you that? That it upsets him?

No response.

Ellis   Well he should be upset.

Ayeesha   Wow.

Ellis   I've not forgiven him. And I've definitely not forgotten.

Ayeesha   Not my place to talk about it.

Ellis   You're right, it's not.

Beat.

Ellis   He'll never say sorry.

Ayeesha   And you will?

Ellis   But he's my dad. He's supposed to be the better one.

Ayeesha   You need to give him a bit of grace. You can whine about your relationship with him but are you going to do anything about it? You can't expect him to do everything. He's not perfect but neither are you darling. I think he's a good dad.

Beat.

Ayeesha   He's good with Mia.

Ellis   Yeah. I see that.

Ellis *considers leaving*.

Ayeesha   Would you like to hold her?

No response.

Ayeesha   You don't have to.

Ellis   I'm okay.

Ayeesha   She's your sister, Ellis. I hope you see it that way.

Ellis   I know, I know. I do.

Max enters.

Max   Your mam's asking after you.

Ayeesha   Thank you.

Ayeesha *exits with the baby carrier.*

Max   Is she gone?

Ellis   I think so. You okay?

Max   No. You've seen it now. What she's like.

Ellis   It's not your fault, Max.

Max   It is. And it's her fault. It's all our fault. No one cares about each other in this family. And that'll never change.

Max *goes to leave.*

Ellis   Max.

Max   What?

Ellis   I'm sorry.

Max   For what?

Ellis   I lied. I was being a dick. I do like you. And not just 'cos we're family. I'm sorry.

Ellis *hugs* **Max**.

David *enters.*

David   You good Max-a-million?

Max *nods and exits.*

David   Thanks for coming today.

Ellis   I didn't know you and Grandma weren't talking.

David   She's been civil at odd get togethers and that but generally she hasn't really come anywhere near us. I mean obviously that year we got married, we couldn't see her for months. We moved a bit further out when I lost my job. Then she didn't want to do Christmas at hers anymore. She sent a card when Mia was born but it felt passive aggressive more than anything. It's all just stupid. Petty. I shouldn't have said all that, I shouldn't have told her to leave. This whole thing has gone on too long and I'm not having it anymore.

Ellis   She won't listen to you.

David   Yeah well the least I can do is try, Ellis.

Ellis   Are you mad at me? About Aunty Jacqui?

David   No.

Ellis   I should've said /

David   I wouldn't have wanted to get involved. I'm glad she had someone.

Beat.

David   Your Grandma won't recover from this.

Ellis   From what?

David   Aunty Jacqui.

Ellis   But she hated her.

David   No, she didn't. She was just too proud. I know what she's like. I know how her brain works. This will hit her more than when dad died.

Beat.

David   I didn't know whether or not you were coming today.

Ellis   I thought you'd assume I would be.

David   I'd never assume that.

Beat.

Ellis   Truthfully I came 'cos I needed to tell you something. And if I don't say this now, I don't think I ever will.

David   Alright.

Ellis   I'm pissed off. I'm always pissed off at you. And it's turning me into a miserable person. We never talk about anything, you know, properly. But I want to talk about this.

David   Go on.

Ellis   You don't say that you love me.

David   I do. What you on about?

Ellis   You don't, Dad. You stopped doing it. And I don't know if it's a conscious thing or it's a part of me growing up but I started to notice it after I came out to you. And it's hard 'cos I crave this validation. This validation from you, from Grandma. And I get why you struggled, I do. I try not to hold that against you. But it's been thirteen years and I don't get why you can't just be happy for me.

David   I am happy for you.

Ellis   You don't show it. You don't say it.

David   I don't feel the need to share everything.

Ellis   But I feel the need. What about what I need?

David   What do you need?

Ellis   I need to feel like my own dad is proud of me.

David   I've always been proud of you, Ellis. Don't take that away from me. I'm the one who found money where there wasn't any and paid for dance lessons every week, who paid for costumes for competitions. Always on the front row, always the one cheering the loudest.

Ellis　But that's me being a dancer. You don't really like me that much.

David　That's ridiculous.

Ellis　You don't though. Not how you like Max.

David　Don't be jealous of Max, you know it's not been easy for them.

Ellis　Was it easy for me?

A moment.

David　I know it wasn't. You don't have to tell me that.

Ellis　I've never forgiven you.

David　What?

Ellis　That day I told you. You didn't say anything to me. You watched me cry and didn't say anything. You got up and walked away. I don't have a mam and when I came out, you made me feel like I no longer had a dad.

A moment.

David　I don't speak a lot so I'm just going to say my piece.

Ellis　Okay.

David　I know you resent me and think I'm this terrible dad.

Ellis　I don't think that.

David　You do and that's alright. You can sometimes be a twat so we're sort of even there. But I deserve a second chance to be better. Well I'd like to think I do. And I don't just mean with Mia.

Beat.

David　I've been thinking a lot about the family. About my dad. He lost me a long time ago, well before he died. Yeah, we stayed in eachothers lives but we stopped meaning something to each other. I don't want that. I don't want you to see me die and not have it mean something. I get it, I get it Ellis. We clash. I say the wrong things 'cos how I was raised. That's the world I grew up in. But that's not an excuse. I don't want you to change, I'm not going to. But I'd change how I was if I could. I want you here. This is your family. You're my son. I am proud of you. And I love you.

Ellis   I love you too, Dad.

A moment.

David   I haven't done the thing.

Ellis   The thing?

David   I haven't asked.

Ellis   Ah. You haven't.

David   Well? Do you need any money?

Ellis   No.

David   Have you done anything illegal?

Ellis   No.

David   Good. Are you seeing anyone?

Beat.

Ellis   Yeah. Yeah I am actually.

David   What's his name?

Ellis   Damien.

David   Is he nice?

Ellis   Yeah, really nice.

David   Do you love him?

Ellis   Jesus. I've been seeing him for two months, Dad.

David   Alright, alright. Well it's Ayeesha's 40th next month so if it's alright, I'd like to meet Damien.

Ellis   Okay.

David   Son?

Ellis   Yeah.

David   I know you don't like when I do this but it's important to me. Next time when I call, will you please answer the phone?

Ellis   I will.

David *grabs* **Ellis**'s *shoulder and squeezes it.*

A moment.

They hug.

David   Come on. I want you to hold your sister.

David *exits but* **Ellis** *lingers.*

He surveys the room.

Before leaving, he picks up something from the buffet.

He eats it and exits.

Black out.

The End.

Printed in the USA
CPSIA information can be obtained
at www.ICGtesting.com
LVHW021146090324
773943LV00002B/313

9 781350 454576